HONEST TO MAN

Christian Ethics Re-examined

Honest to Man

Christian Ethics Re-examined

MARGARET KNIGHT

PROMETHEUS BOOKS, BUFFALO, NY

First published 1974 by Elek Books Ltd, London,
in association with Pemberton Books
(Pemberton Publishing Co Ltd), London
and Prometheus Books,
923 Kensington Avenue, Buffalo, NY 14215

SBN 0 87975 029 4

Printed in Great Britain

CONTENTS

Part III CHRISTIANITY TODAY

PREFACE

The climate of thought regarding religion has changed profoundly in the last two decades. When, in 1955, I gave two broadcasts entitled 'Morals without Religion', in which I expressed scepticism about the traditional Christian doctrines, I was subjected to a storm of abuse: today, similar views are expressed by Anglican bishops and nobody turns a hair. The fashionable view at the present time is that the important thing about Christianity is not its cosmology but its ethic. Protestant Churchmen admit cheerfully that most of the statements in the creeds are only 'symbolically' true, but they maintain none the less that Christianity is profoundly important and that it is essential to preserve it in some form, since—to quote Lady Stocks in a recent *Any Questions* programme—'the best expression of a moral order the world has yet had is the Christian one'.

In the nineteen-fifties I was inclined to share this view, and in my broadcasts I argued simply that it was a mistake to tie a live ethic to a dying theology. But it dawned on me later that my admiration for Christian ethics was based mainly on an inadequate knowledge of the Gospels, combined with the slanted view of history that I, like most of my generation, had acquired at school. Wider reading has now convinced me that there is no ground for the common claim that Christianity is the source of all that is best in our culture. The true roots of our civilization, I now believe, lie in classical Greece and Rome: and I believe too that it was one of the major disasters of history when Europe turned aside from its true heritage to embrace an ascetic, other-worldly religion which for centuries has served to stifle the free intelligence and to limit disastrously the range of human sympathies.

The present book states my grounds for this belief. I shall doubtless be told that it is one-sided, and this is of course undeniable—the book is one-sided in the sense in which a speech by prosecuting counsel is one-sided. But in view of the hundreds of books that are written each year from the standpoint of defending counsel, it seems reasonable that the other side should be heard.

There is a tendency in some quarters to seek always for common ground between opposing views, and to assume without question that the 'mature' attitude is to adopt a position midway between them. I must confess to a lack of sympathy with this assumption. The function of judge and jury, after all, is not to find common ground between the defence and the prosecution but to decide which has the better case: and the aim of this book is to convince readers that, in the issues with which it is concerned, the balance of truth lies with the prosecution.

The book makes no claim to be a work of original research. Readers may find some of the facts it contains to be unfamiliar and surprising, but this is not usually because they are inaccessible—most of them can be readily found in standard histories and works of reference by those who are willing to look—but because they are habitually underemphasized. Among the many historical sources that I have consulted I must acknowledge a special debt to *The History of European Morals from Augustus to Charlemagne* by W. E. H. Lecky—a nineteenth century historian who in style and erudition can reasonably be compared with Macaulay, but who incurred *odium theologicum* in his lifetime through the frankness with which he described the social effects of Christianity.

Parts of Chapter 9 of this book have already appeared in my article 'Morality—Supernatural or Social?' in *The Humanist Outlook*, edited by Professor A. J. Ayer. My thanks are due to the Pemberton Publishing Company for permission to reprint. Thanks are also due to Messrs Collins for permission to quote the passage on pages 13 to 15 from Robert Ardrey's *African Genesis*.

MARGARET KNIGHT

Aberdeen, 1973

PART I

CHRISTIAN AND HUMANIST ETHICS

ONE

INTRODUCTION

The Catholic Bishop of Salford wrote in 1956 'For the vast mass of modern men the teaching of religious truth and the consequences of divine revelation are simply irrelevant to the question of living. . . . The Church, at least as a teacher, is just another museum piece, a milestone at the side of the road along which mankind has passed in its onward march.'[1]

In the years that have passed since this was written, its truth has become increasingly evident. Resignations from the priesthood are increasing and ordinations falling away. Baptisms and confirmations are becoming steadily fewer, and in England less than 15 per cent of the population goes regularly to church.* It is true that, as opinion polls have shown, most people in Britain still describe themselves as Christians; but the majority are using the term Christian in a sense so nebulous that they themselves cannot say what they mean by it. They are unlikely to mean that they believe the world was created by an omnipotent and benevolent Spirit, who two thousand years ago manifested himself briefly in human form in one of the remoter provinces of the Roman Empire.

Many older people, of course, still accept unquestioningly the beliefs they were taught in childhood. But by the time the generation now at school is in charge of

---

* This figure includes Roman Catholics, who attend church far more regularly than Protestants.

affairs, it is likely that what Newman so justly termed 'the all-corroding, all-dissolving scepticism of the intellect in religious inquiries'[2] will have completed its work, and doctrinal Christianity will be no more than a historical survival. To the Humanist, of course, this is ground for satisfaction, but many people find the prospect deeply alarming. This is not necessarily because they are orthodox Christians; but they feel that, even though Christian theology must now be regarded as largely 'symbolic', to use the fashionable term, the Christian ethic is the highest the world has known and the source of all that is best in our civilization. And they feel, too, that the ethic is in some sense dependent on the theology—that without belief in some kind of supernatural authority the whole basis of morals would collapse. So they argue that some semblance, at least, of Christian belief must be maintained in order to make people good; and they feel, though they do not always say so explicitly, that the only effective way to achieve this is to instil Christian belief into children at school when they are too young to be critical.

The main purpose of the present book is to suggest that these attitudes are mistaken; that morality needs no supernatural sanction, and that the philosophical arguments which claim to show that it does, are fallacious; that the mainsprings of moral action are what Darwin called the social instincts—tendencies towards altruism and co-operation that are as much part of our innate biological equipment as are our tendencies towards aggression and cruelty; that Jesus of Nazareth had many human failings, and was by no means the flawless character that the Church depicts him; that the ethic he taught, far from being the source of all that is best in our civilization, was radically defective and has done more harm than good in the course of history; and that the attempt to preserve moral standards by indoctrinating children with Christianity leads to a pervasive intellectual dishonesty and is in any case doomed to failure.

TWO

MORALITY AND THE SOCIAL INSTINCTS

Those who still cling to orthodox Christianity are often people who feel strongly about right and wrong, and who have been taught to think that these concepts have no meaning apart from God. One of the leading exponents of the 'no good without God' argument was that most popular of Christian apologists the late C. S. Lewis, who in his book *Mere Christianity*[1] argued the case so persuasively that it is difficult for the ordinary reader to see where the fallacy lies. But the argument undoubtedly is fallacious, and one need not be a trained logician to understand why this is so.

Stripped down to essentials, the argument runs as follows. Human beings would have no ground for trusting their judgments about what things are good or evil, or what actions are right or wrong, unless they believed that these judgments are backed by an authority that is more than human. However much we may disagree about specific moral issues, most of us accept without question such basic ethical principles as that love is better than hate, and that kindness is better than cruelty. But how do we know that in stating such principles we are doing anything more than expressing our personal preferences? According to C. S. Lewis the only justifiable ground for our confidence is the belief that these, like all other ethical principles, reflect the preferences of a superhuman authority whom we call God.

But the argument will not stand up to logical criticism. The sceptic may reasonably ask why we should be guided by God's preferences—to which the believer can only reply that it is because what God prefers is good. But what exactly does this statement mean? Does God prefer certain things because they are good? Or are certain things called good because God prefers them? If he opts for the first alternative, the believer implies that he has knowledge of good that is not dependent on his knowledge of God's preferences. If he opts for the second, he is saying in effect that the word 'good' *means* 'preferred by God'—so that the statement that God prefers what is good amounts to no more than that God prefers what he prefers, which is a tautology.

Professor A. J. Ayer makes this point with his usual lucidity. He writes:

No doubt the premiss that what God wills is right is one that religious believers take for granted. The fact remains that even if they were justified in making this assumption, it implies that they have a standard of morality which is independent of their belief in God. The proof of this is that when they say that God is good or that he wills what is right, they surely do not mean merely to express the tautology that he is what he is or that he wills what he wills. If they did mean no more than this, they would be landed with the absurd consequence that even if the actions of the deity were such as, in any other person, we should characterize as those of a malignant demon, they would still, by definition, be right. But the fact is that believers in God think of the goodness which they attribute to him as something for which we ought to be grateful. Now this would make no sense at all

2

if the deity's volition set the standard of value: for in that case, no matter what he was understood to will, we should still be obliged to think him good.[2]

Thus the Humanist rejects the belief that terms like 'good' and 'right' must inevitably, in the last analysis, imply a reference to God. And he holds, further, that the belief in question is not only mistaken but, in a quite literal sense, childish. It provides a close analogy with the attitude of the young child, to whom 'good' means simply what pleases the grown-ups and 'bad' means what makes them angry. To borrow an example from Professor Nowell-Smith:[3] to the small boy the reason he must not pull his sister's hair is that Mummy will be angry, or that Mummy will punish him. He has made a considerable step forward towards maturity of moral judgment when he realizes that the fundamental reason for not pulling his sister's hair is that it hurts her. There is a similar step forward in the morality of communities when men outgrow the belief that morality consists simply in blind obedience to authority, and realize that, essentially, to act rightly is to act for the common good.

The contrast highlights the basic difference between Christian and Humanist morality. To the orthodox Christian, morality is authoritarian—to act rightly is to act in accordance with God's will. To the Humanist, morality is a social matter—to act rightly is to act in a way that increases well-being and happiness, and/or reduces avoidable suffering, among conscious* beings. However,

---

* The adjective 'conscious' is here used in preference to 'human' so as to avoid the impression that Humanists are indifferent to the well-being of animals. But for simplicity's sake the word 'human' will usually be used hereafter.

Christianity today has become appreciably less authoritarian, and many liberal Christians would now accept the
Humanist view, up to a point. They would agree that
right and wrong are to be defined in terms of human well-
being; but they would say that without belief in God we
should have no motive for wanting to promote human
well-being—that an atheist is being completely inconsistent if he ever behaves unselfishly or ever considers anyone's interest but his own. The late Father Ronald Knox
had a pleasing phrase about 'this Something which
underwrites all the dictates of conscience, hamstrings the
mind with hesitations when there is a blow to be struck
for self-interest, reinforces the claims of altruism and sends
us back to the tail of the queue'.[4] Humanists fully admit
the existence of this something, but they do not, like
Father Knox, spell it with a capital S and equate it with
God. There is no more need to postulate a personal God
to account for altruism than a personal Devil to account
for aggression. There is a quite simple explanation of why
people often behave unselfishly. Man is a social animal,
and like the members of all other social species, he has
tendencies towards co-operation and altruism that are
just as instinctive*—just as biologically primary—as his
tendencies towards aggression. This conflicts with the
view, which is still quite widely held, that aggression and
co-operation are biologically on different levels—that
aggressive behaviour is innate while co-operative behaviour occurs only as a result of social training or
religious belief.

---

* I use the unfashionable term 'instinct' without apology, as it is
less cumbrous than the various current alternatives such as 'built-in
response tendency' or 'unlearned motivation', and it does not, so far
as I can see, in any way differ from them in meaning.

Recent work on the so-called lower animals is relevant here, and it will now be necessary to make a short excursion into zoology—which, however, will all lead back to the human species in the end. Everyone is familiar with the classification of animal species into gregarious or non-gregarious—the gregarious or social species being those, such as apes, wolves or seals, who lead a communal life in troops, packs or herds, and the non-gregarious being those, such as foxes, for whom the basic unit is simply the family unit of fox, vixen and cubs, and who do not form wider groupings. But what is not so universally realized is the amount of co-operative, altruistic behaviour that occurs among gregarious species. Even non-gregarious animals, of course, are co-operative towards their mates and offspring, but among gregarious species the area of co-operation is far wider. This is by no means a new discovery, but until recently it was an unfashionable truth, largely because behaviouristically-minded psychologists preferred experimenting with animals in laboratories to observing them in their natural state; and in laboratories (and even, to a lesser extent, in zoos) the opportunities for the display of animal sociality are limited. In consequence the crucial part played by such sociality in the wild state went unrecognized. To quote Robert Ardrey:

> In zoos there are no predators and there is no fear. And all those delicate instinctual mechanisms evolved by natural selection to promote the survival of individuals or the survival of species are alike suspended. Only sex and a hearty appetite remain for us to see. But how delicate may be the instinctual social responses in a state of nature has been recorded by many an observer.[5]

After the Second World War, however, there was an upsurge of interest in ethology—the study of animal species in their wild state—and from that time onwards there has been a spate of books and articles on the social behaviour of animals, particularly that of our nearest relatives, the apes and monkeys. Thus a well-known study of baboons by Washburn and De Vore[6] describes how when a troop of baboons moves from place to place—for example from their sleeping-place to a feeding-ground or water-hole—they move always in a certain rough formation, with the smaller juveniles and the mothers with infants in the centre. If a predator is sighted the adult males immediately move around so as to form a defensive phalanx between it and the more vulnerable members of the group. Again, baby baboons are objects of great interest and solicitude, not only to their own parents, but to the whole community. Any adult baboon will act protectively towards a young one when necessary, whether or not it is its own offspring. For example, if a group of young baboons are playing together and the play becomes rough and one of them is hurt and cries out, any adult within hearing will intervene to protect the victim and quieten the others.

Among apes and monkeys in the wild state there is very little serious fighting. This fact caused great surprise to the first ethologists, since earlier views of primate society had been based largely on study of animals in captivity. In these conditions such communities as could be formed were usually no more than anarchic and quarrelsome mobs. But when field workers began to study apes and monkeys in their natural state, one after another found that the particular species he was observing was remarkably peaceful. The earlier view was at first so deeply

entrenched that each worker was inclined to suppose that
his or her species was unique. But gradually the conclusion dawned that all ape and monkey species are peaceable
in the wild state. They become aggressive only when they
are exposed to stress; and the principal stress that made
them so aggressive in captivity was overcrowding—a fact
that may have its implications for the human species.

In recent years there have been many fascinating television programmes on the social animals, and these have
done much to remove popular misconceptions about the
'law of the jungle'. Animal communities in their natural
state are often friendly and co-operative to an extent that
many human communities would do well to imitate.
This is not to say that aggressive behaviour never occurs;
but aggression between two groups seldom goes beyond
a threatening display near the boundary between their
respective territories, and fights between members of the
same group are seldom more than ritual combats, conducted with a maximum of noise and display and a
minimum of injury. Such fights usually end with one of
the combatants accepting defeat, and signalling the fact
by a submissive gesture such as rolling on his back—on
which the victor makes no attempt to press his advantage,
but simply withdraws from the conflict.

Among apes and monkeys, when serious conflict
threatens within the group it is usually stopped immediately by the leader or some other high-ranking member of
the band. To quote from a broadcast 'Violence, Monkeys
and Man' by W. M. S. Russell:

> Leaders play a vital part in monkey societies. Their
> experience is valuable in seeking food and avoiding
> danger. In grave emergency, they come out fearlessly

from central headquarters to defend any citizens threatened by predators. But their chief function, almost the defining function of primate leaders, is the reduction of violence, including their own, to an absolute minimum. In all primate species, when quarrels threaten within the band, they are at once stopped by the intervention of the leader, supported by the establishment, who never quarrel among themselves.[7]

('The establishment' is Russell's humorous term for the high-status members who rank just below the leader.)

In emergencies that threaten the group, animal leaders are capable of behaviour which in human beings would be described as heroic self-sacrifice. Here Robert Ardrey may be quoted once more. His dramatic description is based on observations made by the South African biologist Eugene Marais in an area known as the Waterberg.

[In the Waterberg] night comes on like a silent express train, and the dark becomes quiet with the listening of animals. In the hour before dusk baboon troops throughout all Marais' area would come scampering back from their scattered feeding grounds to the security of home and numbers. One fortunate troop, for example, slept in an almost inaccessible cave five hundred feet high on a sheerest cliff. There was a way to the cave, a ledge half a mile long and in places only six inches wide that over-hung like the cave itself a fall as fatal for baboons as for baboon enemies. In the hour before nightfall the ledge would be crowded with the troop seeking safety. Marais would watch, and marvel at the orderly movement. Caution for once stilled baboon chatter. Adult males led, then childless females, then females to whose backs and bellies clung infants. . . . At last the cave would fill, and the ledge would clear. Night would fall, and death would move on unheard feet through wood and bush and clearing. . . . But at least one society of animals was safe, and would sleep in peace.

Other troops in the Waterberg, such as Marais' own, possessed no strongholds of comparable strength. Yet to all, whatever their insecurity, night brought the same spectre. Marais could always tell when a leopard was in the neighbourhood of his own band. Protected by nothing but the rocky hollows in the krans and concealed only by the limbs of the massive wild fig, the troop would begin to move uneasily. He would sense the restlessness, and then hear a particular cry of disturbance. Helplessly the troop would wait for unseen death to pass unseeing. But one night the leopard came early.

It was still dusk. The troop had only just returned from the feeding grounds and had barely time to reach its scattered sleeping places in the high-piled rocks behind the fig tree. Now it shrilled its terror. And Marais could see the leopard. It appeared from the bush and took its insolent time. So vulnerable were the baboons that the leopard seemed to recognize no need for hurry. He crouched just below a little jutting cliff observing his prey and the problems of the terrain. And Marais saw two male baboons edging along the cliff above him.

The two males moved cautiously. The leopard, if he saw them, ignored them. His attention was fixed on the swarming, screeching, defenceless horde scrambling among the rocks. Then the two males dropped. They dropped on him from a height of twelve feet. One bit at the leopard's spine. The other struck at his throat while clinging to his neck from below. In an instant the leopard disembowelled with his hind claws the

baboon hanging to his neck and caught in his jaws the
baboon on his back. But it was too late. The dying,
disembowelled baboon had hung on just long enough
and had reached the leopard's jugular vein with his
canines.

Marais watched while the movement stilled beneath
the little jutting cliff. Night fell. . . . And in the hollow
places in the rocky, looming krans a society of animals
settled down to sleep.[8]

These primate heroes were not acting from religious
conviction. Their self-sacrifice provides a particularly
dramatic example of what behaviourist psychologists
would call built-in group-survival responses, and the
layman might prefer to describe as instinctive altruism.
Whatever term is used, the behaviour it denotes was
clearly spontaneous. And it raises the obvious question—
since social animals are so clearly capable of spontaneous
self-sacrifice in the interests of the community, why
should we deny the same capacity to man?

Such a denial would involve, in effect, denying that
man is by nature a gregarious species. Obviously he
behaves gregariously now; but it can be argued, though
very unplausibly, that the tendency to socialized, co-
operative behaviour is not built in to human beings as it is
into apes and seals—not something that comes naturally
in certain circumstances just as aggression comes naturally
in others—but something that has been laboriously
imposed by religion or social training on man's natural
tendency to be entirely selfish, or at least to be unselfish
only towards sexual partners and offspring. If this view
were correct it would imply that our primitive ancestors
were non-gregarious, and many people believe that this
is so—influenced, perhaps, by childhood stories about

'primitive cave men' who were visualized as solitary hunters. But anthropology gives no support to these stories. On the contrary, there is abundant evidence that our earliest human ancestors lived in communities, as did also the ape-men or hominids from whom they descended. In the words of Professor Le Gros Clark 'consciously directed co-operativeness has been the major factor which determined the evolutionary origin of *homo sapiens* as a newly emergent species'.[9]

This is not to deny that our primitive ancestors were often aggressive, just as we ourselves are. 'Natural' behaviour, both among animals and primitive man, involves co-operation within the troop, herd or kinship group (the 'in-group', in modern sociological parlance), and non-co-operation, and in some cases aggression, towards the 'out-group'. But the essential fact is that the co-operative and aggressive tendencies are biologically on a level. Both are built-in; both manifest themselves spontaneously in appropriate circumstances; and both, doubtless, were necessary for man's survival in the primitive state. But in the highly-organized community life of today, it is desirable that the social or co-operative tendencies should be strengthened, and the aggressive tendencies kept to a large extent under control. Indeed it could be argued that the very survival of *homo sapiens* depends on the success of this process—more specifically, on the extent to which we succeed in increasing the size of the in-group within which people spontaneously co-operate, while formalizing and ritualizing the expression of aggression towards out-groups. But this is a topic too vast to consider here.

It must be emphasized that calling behaviour 'innate' or 'instinctive' does not imply that it cannot be modified.

Certain basic tendencies have been built in to the human species, but the expression of these tendencies is progressively elaborated, controlled and modified by environmental pressures, until by the time a person becomes adult his behaviour is scarcely ever purely instinctive—it is the expression of instinct modified by learning. In every human community certain potentialities are encouraged and developed and certain others played down—a fact which is now commonly expressed by saying that every community has its characteristic pattern of culture.

The extent to which these culture-patterns may differ has been vividly brought out by social anthropologists working among primitive people. Where co-operation and aggression are concerned, the extremes are probably represented by the Arapesh of New Guinea and the Kwakiutl of Vancouver Island. Among the Arapesh, described by Margaret Mead,[10] every possible activity, such as building one's house or cultivating one's garden, was performed in friendly co-operation with neighbours and relatives; and aggression was so rare, and so strongly discountenanced, that grown men would burst into tears at an unkind word. At the other extreme were the Kwakiutl, described by Ruth Benedict,[11] among whom the avowed aim of hospitality was to humiliate and embarrass one's guests, and where an accepted way of dealing with personal grief, such as bereavement, was to kill some member of an out-group who was quite unconnected with it—a procedure known as 'killing to wipe one's eyes'.

It is sometimes argued, as against the view that the social instincts are innate, that the cruelties of the Second World War showed how human beings 'naturally' behave when the restraints of religion are removed. A reply *ad hominem* would be that the Christians in the ages of faith behaved far more cruelly than the Nazis, so that religion cannot in itself be a prophylactic against cruelty—indeed it may greatly encourage it if, like medieval Christianity, it involves the belief in a God who tortures his enemies. But in more general terms the answer to the argument is simply this. A community that sets out to increase aggression will almost certainly get results, just as will a community that sets out to reduce it; but there is no reason to suppose that the extreme cruelty that can be produced by the one kind of training is any more 'natural' than the extreme co-operativeness that can be produced by the opposite kind.

Even the most aggressive human communities show considerable co-operation within the in-group. One of the most effective ways of promoting aggression towards out-groups is to break down, as far as possible, all sense of common humanity between the aggressors and their victims. Thus the Nazis were systematically trained to regard the Jews as an inferior species beyond the pale of human sympathy—with the result that concentration camp guards could drive Jews into the gas-chambers with no more compunction than is (presumably) felt by slaughterhouse workers driving cattle into an abattoir. But it would be extravagantly pessimistic to suggest that this is 'natural' human behaviour—the sort of thing we should all like to do if we had not been trained and conditioned to think it wrong. Those concentration camp guards who were not perverts and sadists to begin with had to undergo considerable indoctrination before they would do what was required of them, and even so, some broke down under the strain and a few even committed suicide. Horace's dictum that you can expel nature with a fork but that she will always return again applies to our natural social tendencies as much as to any others.

The survival value of co-operation has already been emphasized, and the point is worth making that one of the first to recognize this was Darwin. Many will find this fact surprising, since Darwin's views are still often misunderstood. It is widely supposed that his theory of evolution by natural selection implies a constant struggle for survival between individuals. If this were so, self-centred aggression would have high survival value, and co-operation would be dysgenic. But this was not in fact Darwin's view. He held that the evolutionary struggle takes place primarily between groups or communities rather than individuals; and, clearly, one of the main factors making for the survival of a community is a high degree of co-operation and mutual aid. In the fourth chapter of *The Descent of Man* Darwin accumulated examples of co-operative behaviour among social animals, and remarked very reasonably, 'It can hardly be disputed that the social feelings are instinctive or innate in the lower animals; and why should they not be so in man?' He concluded the chapter with what may be regarded as the classical statement of the Humanist view on the social basis of morals. 'The social instincts—the prime principle of man's moral constitution—with the aid of active intellectual powers and the effects of habit, naturally lead to the golden rule, "As ye would that men should do to you, do ye to them likewise;" and this lies at the foundation of morality.'

The fact that man is a social animal was taken for granted in the great Humanist civilizations of the pre-Christian era, such as China in the 6th to 3rd centuries BC, and in classical Greece and Rome. Thus Seneca wrote:

'We are members of one great body. Nature has made us
relatives. . . . She planted in us a mutual love, and fitted
us for a social life.'[12] Cicero wrote, 'Men were born for
the sake of men, that each should assist the others,'[13] and
again, 'Nature has inclined us to love men, and this is the
foundation of the law.'[14]

The traditional Christian view, by contrast, is that
fallen man is by nature completely selfish, and that he can
be induced to behave altruistically only through the grace
of God, and the influence of supernatural rewards and
punishments. The Anglican prayer book proclaims that
we are all 'miserable sinners', that there is 'no health in us'
and that 'through the weakness of our mortal nature we
can do no good thing without thee'. Many present-day
Christians have expounded the same depressing view.
Thus Professor Basil Willey maintains that altruism is
'theoretically indefensible except on religious presupposi-
tions'.[15] Mr Christopher Hollis has said: 'Nothing could
be more false than the notion that something in the nature
of the Christian's duty to one's neighbour is a duty
universally self-evident. On the contrary, it is a derivation
from the acceptance of the duty towards God, and, unless
the primary duty is accepted, there is little reason to accept
the secondary duty.'[16] The Bishop of Southwark has proclaimed, more briefly, that 'Christianity is the supreme
reason why men and women should lead decent lives'.[17]
And the Rev. Andrew Morton, Chaplain of Edinburgh
University, said recently in a television programme, in
the tones of one stating a truism, that 'we do not naturally
act compassionately'.

These statements are fully in accordance with Gospel
teaching, as will be illustrated in Chapter 4. Through
its failure to realize that man is a social animal, the

Christian religion has been led throughout most of its history to proclaim, and practise, a code of morality that is in essence completely self-interested. It has denied and discouraged man's natural social tendencies and encouraged a self-centred preoccupation with one's own virtue and one's own salvation. These may appear to be strong statements, but they will be amply supported by evidence in the historical chapters that follow.

THREE

THE PERSONALITY OF JESUS

Many Humanists who have been involved in 'dialogue', to use the now fashionable word, with Christians, must have had the experience of quoting from the Gospels in support of their case and getting the astonished reply 'But surely *that's* not in the Bible!' It would seem that most people today—even those who are still professing Christians—have scarcely opened a New Testament since their schooldays. They are familiar with a few passages that they have heard read again and again at school assembly and in Church, and they tacitly assume that these passages are typical. But this is by no means always the case.

It must be remembered, of course, that the Gospels are second or third-hand accounts written thirty years or more after the events they purport to describe, so that it would be rash to assume that any of the statements they attribute to Jesus contain his actual words. (This proviso should be borne in mind whenever in what follows reference is made to 'Jesus' words' or to 'what Jesus said'). But it seems reasonable to make the same assumption about the Gospel sayings as is made, for example, about the *Analects* of Confucius—that though they are far from being verbatim reports, they do, taken together, give a substantially accurate picture of the speaker's personality and the general tenor of his teaching. If we make this assumption, and if we read the Gospels as a whole instead of in the highly selective way in which we are encouraged to read them, we shall find that they depict the founder of Christianity, not as the traditional 'gentle Jesus', but as a complex and baffling character, at times gentle and affectionate and at others intolerant, vindictive and harsh.

Theologians, who have a professional duty to read the Gospels as a whole, come to them with the long-since-formed assumption that they depict a perfect character; and when they are confronted with what they sometimes euphemistically describe as 'the darker lines in the picture', they employ three main techniques to soften their impact. One method is simply to ignore the troublesome statements; another to try to explain them away as 'symbolic'; and the third to say that the statements in question are so obviously out of character that they must be the result of misreporting or mistranslation.

For example: the first method (ignoring) is applied to the injunction to hate one's family quoted on p. 32; the second method (explaining away as symbolic) is applied, by Protestants though not by Catholics, to Jesus' repeated threats of eternal torment for sinners and unbelievers (cf p. 38); and the third method (explaining away as misreporting) is applied to the curious episode, described in all three synoptic Gospels,* in which the disciples ask Jesus why he speaks to them in parables and receive the reply that it is so that they (the disciples) shall understand him and that unbelievers shall not; since if the latter understood his message they might be converted and their sins

---

* This term is applied to the Gospels of Matthew, Mark and Luke (of which Mark is in fact the earliest) which have a great deal in common and which clearly derive from a common source.

be forgiven them* (Matt. xiii, 10–17, Mark iv, 11–12, Luke viii, 9–10). This has defeated all attempts at 'symbolic' interpretation, and the explanation usually offered is that Mark (later uncritically followed by Matthew and Luke) had confused Jesus' teaching with that of the so-called 'mystery religions' (cf p. 55), which were widespread in the Greco-Roman world, and whose esoteric doctrines were revealed only to initiates. 'Mark's theory' says *The Interpreter's Bible* 'can only be described as perverse'.

But clearly these techniques cannot be justified. If we read the biography of a complex character who said many inspiring things and also many things that were shocking, we should not think it reasonable to dismiss all the shocking things as spurious on the ground that they were inconsistent with the inspiring things that he said at other times. A hostile critic might with equal justification select on the opposite principle, accepting the shocking statements as genuine and rejecting the inspiring ones.

Moreover, these apologetic techniques, which are applied to the reported doings as well as to the sayings of Jesus, have obvious dangers for Christian orthodoxy. Christian doctrinal claims, after all, rest solely on the authority of the Gospels; there is no other source. So the more eager Christians are to assert that such-and-such statements in the Gospels were not meant to be taken literally, and that such-and-such other statements were meant literally but were in fact mistaken, the more difficult it becomes to accept, on the authority of the Gospels

---

* A similar suggestion is made by Paul. 'God shall send them strong delusion that they should believe a lie: that they all might be damned who believed not the truth, but had pleasure in unrighteousness' (II Thess. ii, 11–12).

alone, such intrinsically improbable statements as that
Jesus was the son of God, that he rose from the dead, and
that human beings survive the death of the body. And,
whatever some fashionable apologists may say, to abandon
these beliefs is to abandon Christianity.

But to return to the personality of Jesus. Clearly the
Jesus of the Gospels is very different from the Jesus of
tradition. In his preaching he continually extolled loving-
kindness and meekness, but, as so often happens, his
practice fell short of his precepts. He did, it is true, show
warmth and affection towards his disciples and towards
those who took him at his own valuation: and he was
tolerant towards self-confessed sinners. But he was a
fanatic; and, like most fanatics, he could not tolerate
disagreement or criticism. He reacted furiously to the
villages in his native Galilee that were unimpressed by his
teaching. 'Woe unto thee, Chorazin! Woe unto thee
Bethsaida! . . . and thou, Capernaum . . . shalt be brought
down to hell. . . . It shall be more tolerable for the land of
Sodom in the day of judgment than for thee' (Matt. xii,
21, 23, 24). Towards the Pharisees in particular, who were
sceptical of his messianic pretensions, he was often
savagely vindictive. Any hint of criticism, any demand
that he should produce evidence for his claims, was liable
to provoke a torrent of wrath and denunciation. Most of
Matthew xxiii, for example, is not, as we are encouraged
to regard it, a lofty and dignified rebuke: it is what on any
other lips would be described as a stream of invective.
'Woe unto you, scribes and Pharisees, hypocrites! for
ye are like unto whited sepulchres, which, indeed,
appear beautiful outward, but are within full of
dead men's bones, and of all uncleanness. . . . Ye
serpents, ye generation of vipers, how can ye escape the

damnation of hell?' This can hardly be called loving one's enemies.

Jesus, in fact, was typical of a certain kind of fanatical young idealist: at one moment holding forth, with tears in his eyes, about the need for universal love; at the next, furiously denouncing the morons, crooks and bigots who do not see eye to eye with him. It is very natural and very human behaviour. But it is not superhuman. Many of the great men of history (for example, Socrates) have met criticism with more dignity and restraint.

Other aspects of Jesus' personality, such as his attitude towards personal relationships, towards sex and marriage and towards the intellect, will be considered in relation to his teaching in the chapter that follows.

FOUR

THE TEACHING OF JESUS

Love and Reward

Jesus' teachings on love and forgiveness are commonly held to have been epoch-making; I have even heard a cleric assert, in the course of a TV discussion, that 'Christianity introduced the word "love" into our language'. But in fact these ideals were not originated by Jesus, and are no way specifically Christian. They were proclaimed by the Humanist philosophers of China in the sixth century BC, and later by the Jews of the pre-Christian era, by the Greek and Roman Stoics, and many others.

Confucius, for example, taught that virtue depends on the combination of wisdom with good feeling—the essence of good feeling being summed up in the word *Jin*, which may be translated as love of one's fellows, goodwill, humanity. (In our own day Bertrand Russell expressed the same attitude when he said that 'the good life is the life inspired by love and guided by knowledge'.) More than once in his writings Confucius proclaimed the Golden Rule 'Do not do to others what you would not like yourself'; and a century earlier the quietist philosopher Lao-Tzu exhorted his followers to 'requite injuries with good deeds'.

As for the Jews—the injunction to love one's neighbour as oneself is to be found in the book of Leviticus (xix, 18), dating from around 400 BC. And an apocryphal book of the second century BC *The Testament of the Twelve Patriarchs* contains ethical teachings that clearly foreshadow, and that probably influenced, the teachings of Jesus and of Paul. The book, as its title implies, was ascribed to the leaders of the twelve tribes of Israel, but it was in fact the work of a single writer, a Pharisee, who apparently regarded John Hyrcanus, the ruler of the Maccabean dynasty, as the expected Messiah. It contains such precepts as the following:

> Love ye one another from the heart; and if a man sin against thee, speak peaceably to him, and in thy soul hold not guile; and if he repent and confess, forgive him. But if he deny it, do not get into a passion with him, lest catching the poison from thee he take to swearing, and so then sin doubly. . . . And if he be shameless and persist in wrong-doing, even so forgive him from the heart, and leave to God the avenging.[1]

Jesus' saying 'He that is without sin among you, let him first cast a stone' (John viii, 7) is revered as one of his most inspired pronouncements, and one of those that most clearly reveal him as a moral innovator. But similar attitudes were frequently expressed by the Stoics. Seneca, for example, wrote in his essay *On Anger*:

> No man of sense will hate the erring; otherwise he will hate himself. Let him reflect how often he himself offends against morality, and how many of his own acts need forgiveness; then he will be angry with himself also. For no just judge will pronounce one sort of judgment in his own case, and a different one in the case of others. No one will be found who can justly acquit himself; anyone who declares himself blameless

is relying on the absence of witnesses rather than the voice of his conscience. How much more human it is to show a kind and fatherly spirit towards wrongdoers. . . . If a man has lost his way and is trespassing over our fields, it is better to put him upon the right path than to drive him out.[2]

Elsewhere in the same essay Seneca gave some advice on avoiding anger.

What is more admirable than to exchange hostility for friendship? . . . If a man speaks angrily to you, make a good-humoured reply. Animosity dies if it is abandoned by one side; it takes two to make a quarrel. . . . If someone strikes you, step back; for by striking back you will give him both the opportunity and the excuse to repeat his blow, and when later you wish to end the quarrel, it will be impossible.[3]

Some Christian apologists have suggested that Seneca must 'really' have been a Christian, and the same claim would probably have been made for the next Stoic writer to be quoted—the Emperor Marcus Aurelius—if his distaste for Christianity had not been so clearly expressed (cf. p. 62).* If the slightly *de haut en bas* tone of the passage that follows makes it at first sight less attractive than Seneca's, it must be remembered that the writer was the most powerful man in the world.

Remember that gentleness is invincible, if it be genuine and not sneering or hypocritical. For what can

---

* Marcus Aurelius is said to have persecuted the Christians. This is probably an overstatement, but it is true that during his reign there was a short outbreak of persecution at Lyons, which he may or may not have condoned.

the most insolent do to you, if you continue gentle to
him, and if opportunity allows, mildly admonish him
and quietly show him a better way at the very moment
when he attempts to do you injury: 'My son, we were
not born for this, to hurt and annoy one another; it
will be your hurt, not mine, my son.' And point out
with tact and on general grounds that this is so, that
not even bees act like that nor the many creatures that
are by nature gregarious. But you must not do it ironi-
cally or as if finding fault, but affectionately and not
feeling the sting in your soul, nor as if you were
lecturing him or desired some bystander to admire you,
but even if others are present, just in the way you
would address him if you were alone.[4]

Clearly, the Gospel ethic was not as revolutionary as it
is held to be. But there is, none the less, one important
difference between the teaching of the pre-Christian
Humanists and of Jesus. The former attached primary
importance to the relation between man and man; Jesus
to the relation between man and God. Confucius and the
Stoics took it for granted that man is a social animal (cf.
pp. 20–1). Jesus, by contrast, seems to have assumed that
there is no such thing as spontaneous benevolence. It is
true that he enjoined his followers to love their neighbours, but the motive put forward was the same as that
for the less natural requirement that they should love their
enemies, namely that such conduct is pleasing to God and
will earn a substantial reward in the life hereafter. The
Gospel view was summarized quite accurately by the
famous Archdeacon Paley, author of *Evidences of
Christianity*, when he defined virtue as 'doing good to
mankind, in obedience to the will of God, and for the sake
of eternal happiness'.[5] The concept of reward pervades

the moral teaching of the Gospels (the word occurs nine times in the sermon on the mount). For example—

Love ye your enemies, and do good, and lend, hoping for nothing again; and your reward shall be great. (Luke vi, 35)

Give, and it shall be given unto you; good measure, pressed down, and shaken together, and running over. (Luke vi, 38)

(Let) thine alms be in secret: and thy Father which seeth in secret himself shall reward thee openly. (Matt. vi, 4)

The Son of Man shall come in the glory of his Father, with his angels; and then he shall reward every man according to his works. (Matt. xvi, 27)

The implication of these statements is that no reward must be expected in this life, but that in the life to come the dividends, so to speak, will come rolling in. The appeal to 'posthumous self-interest', in John Stuart Mill's words, is unmistakable. It fully justifies the attitude of Mrs Fairchild in the Victorian children's classic ('"He that giveth to the poor lendeth to the Lord, and shall be repaid" said Mrs Fairchild, hastily slipping a shilling into the poor woman's hand'). The Stoic maxim that virtue is its own reward is surely more admirable.

Personal Relationships

Liberal Christians today are fond of asserting that the Gospels show an intense concern for personal relationships. But if we read the Gospels as a whole and not selectively, it becomes impossible to maintain this view. On the contrary, human ties are regarded not merely as less important than, but in some cases as a definite obstacle to, the attainment of a right relationship with God. The type of charity that is commended is a sort of impersonal self-denial based on duty rather than affection. It is admirable to give to the poor—to people one does not know and has possibly never seen—but dangerous to get too fond of one's nearest and dearest, since this may distract one from higher things. The Gospels contain some rather startling pronouncements on the latter theme, to which attention is seldom drawn by Christian moralists. For example:

> And every one that hath forsaken houses, or brethren, or sisters, or father, or mother, or wife, or children, or lands, for my name's sake, shall receive an hundredfold, and shall inherit everlasting life.* (Matt. xix, 29)
>
> For I am come to set a man at variance against his father, and the daughter against her mother . . . and a man's foes shall be they of his own household. (Matt. x, 35–6)
>
> If any man come to me, and hate not his father, and mother, and wife, and children, and brethren, and sisters, yea, and his own life also, he cannot be my disciple. (Luke xiv, 26)

It is not suggested that all or most Christians throughout history have conducted their lives on these principles. As W. K. Clifford said 'if men were no better than their religions, the world would be a hell indeed'. The social instincts have been built into us (cf. pp. 9–16) and it is impossible to get rid of them by telling people that they

---

* It is in something of the same spirit that the Roman Catholic church today exhorts novices taking their vows to 'die to the world, to your parents, to your friends, and to yourself, and live alone for Jesus Christ'.

should really be loving an invisible, intangible God rather than their nearest and dearest. But for a period of some two hundred years in the Dark Ages Christian ascetics did their best to rid themselves entirely of their human affections, and some of the horrible results this produced will be considered in Chapter 9.

The Brotherhood of Man

In the first century BC Cicero wrote: 'Those who say that regard should be had for the rights of fellow-citizens, but not of foreigners, would destroy the universal brotherhood of mankind';[6] and two centuries later Marcus Aurelius wrote 'As an Antonine, my country is Rome: as a man, it is the world'.[7] It is claimed for Jesus that he, too, taught the brotherhood of man regardless of race or nation. But in his case the claim is more doubtful.

It is true that Jesus is several times represented as telling the disciples to preach the Gospel 'throughout the world' or 'to all nations'. But one of these statements occurs in a passage (Mark xvi, 9–20) which is generally recognized as a late interpolation, and most of the others are alleged to have been made after the resurrection (Matt. xxviii, 19, Mark xvi, 15, Luke xxiv, 47, Acts i, 8), and this, to a non-Christian, is sufficient reason for doubting their historicity. Some of Jesus' other reported sayings reflect an extreme Jewish exclusiveness: for example: 'Go not into the way of the Gentiles, and into any city of the Samaritans enter ye not: but go rather to the lost sheep of the house of Israel' (Matt. x, 5–6). 'I am not sent but unto the lost sheep of the house of Israel. . . . It is not meet to take the children's bread and to cast it to dogs' (Matt. xv, 24, 26).

In this context, far too much is often made of the

parable of the Good Samaritan; those who quote it seem to assume that the ordinary Jew regarded Samaritans as enemy aliens. But this was not so; Samaria, lying between Judaea and Galilee, was inhabited by a population of mixed descent, with a strong admixture of Jewish blood, whose way of life was predominantly Jewish and who shared the Jewish monotheistic religion. Pure-bred Jews regarded the Samaritans as an inferior race, so for one of them to relate a story in which a Samaritan figured as hero is certainly an indication of broadmindedness. But it can hardly be treated as proof of an international outlook.

All in all, the balance of evidence suggests that Jesus regarded himself simply as the Jewish Messiah. There is little ground for believing that he aspired to convert the world to his Gospel, or to make Gentiles into members of a world-wide Church. These projects derived from Paul rather than Jesus: and Paul's letters (e.g. Galatians ii) show how strongly he was at first opposed by the disciples, who had been with Jesus in his lifetime and so were presumably aware of his views.

Other-worldliness

Jesus was born as a member of a subject people whose country had for some sixty years been occupied and governed by Rome. But the Jewish nation had had a great past, of which it was very conscious, and the tradition prevailed that eventually a deliverer—a Messiah—would come and would restore the lost glories of David and Solomon. The Messianic expectations varied among different sects and in different localities. Some people apparently expected no more than a human resistance leader, who would help them to throw off the yoke of Rome. But the more general expectation, which derived from a tradition dating from long before the Roman occupation, was of a more-or-less supernatural figure—referred to in apocalyptic writings as the Son of Man, a term which Jesus repeatedly applied to himself—who would come to announce the approaching end of the material world and the inauguration of a new, extra-terrestrial Kingdom of God.

If the Gospel statements are to be taken at anything like their face value, there can be no doubt that Jesus, like others before and after him, believed himself to be the expected Messiah; and believed also that the new King-dom, to be inaugurated by his own return to earth and the Last Judgment, was not more than a few years away. He assured his disciples that many of them would still be alive at his Second Coming. 'There be some standing here that shall not taste of death until they see the Son of Man coming in his Kingdom' (Matt. xvi, 28). 'This generation shall not pass till all these things be done' (Mark xiii, 30). When he sent out the disciples to preach he told them that the world would end before they had completed their mission—'Ye shall not have gone over the cities of Israel before the Son of Man be come' (Matt. x, 23). And he exhorted them after he had left them they should live in constant expectation of his return 'Take ye heed, watch and pray: for ye know not when the time is' (Mark xiii, 33) 'Be ye therefore ready: for the Son of Man cometh at an hour when ye think not' (Luke xii, 40).

This expectation profoundly affected Jesus' moral teaching; the ethic he taught was, in Schweitzer's phrase, an *Interimsethik*. He showed no concern for improving the quality of life in this world; the important thing was to ensure one's eternal well-being in the world to come. This attitude, only slightly modified, has persisted throughout almost the whole of the Christian era. One of the principal complaints of the Romans against the early Christians was their lack of any sense of civic responsibility—as the Christian father Tertullian put it 'nothing is of less interest to us than public affairs'.[8] And centuries later, when Christians had ceased to believe that the Last Judgment was imminent, they still showed the same tendency to concern themselves with the next world rather than this.

In Jesus' case this passive, other-worldly attitude was strongly reinforced by political factors. The Jews, as has already been emphasized, were a subject people living under foreign domination. They had almost no power or political responsibility. They were, to put it bluntly, underdogs; and the virtues extolled by Jesus were predominantly the underdog virtues, such as obedience, docility, long-suffering and patience under oppression, rather than the more aristocratic virtues of magnanimity, justice and tolerance which were admired by the Greeks and Romans, but which the Jew of the Roman Empire had little opportunity to practise. It is Jesus' persistent exaltation of the passive virtues which probably explains why, despite the misogynistic attitude that prevailed in the ages of faith (cf. pp. 120-1), Christianity has always appealed more to women than to men.

Jesus' championship of the underdog, however, did not imply that his outlook was egalitarian. The state of affairs which he foretold and to which he looked forward was not one in which privilege was abolished but in which 'first shall be last and the last shall be first' (Matt. xviii, 30) —in other words, in which the privileged and the unprivileged would change places. This attitude is expressed in the Magnificat 'He hath put down the mighty from their seats and exalted them of low degree. He hath filled the hungry with good things; and the rich he hath sent empty away' (Luke i, 52–3). It is of course an excellent thing to feed the hungry, but why—one may ask—starve the rich? This is only perpetuating the present system in reverse. The Gospel accounts suggest that Jesus, despite his preaching of universal love, was not wholly free from the resentment commonly felt by the underdog towards the happier and more fortunate. 'Woe unto ye that are full! for ye shall hunger. Woe unto you that laugh now! for ye shall mourn and weep. Woe unto you when all men shall speak well of you! for so did their fathers to the false prophets' (Luke vi, 25–6).

There are other aspects of Jesus' teaching which can be understood only in their historical context. 'Take no thought for the morrow', for example, becomes less puzzling when we realize that the speaker believed that the world was about to end. 'Resist not evil' and 'turn the other cheek' may well have been good advice to the Palestinian Jew who was being pushed around by the Roman soldiery. But none of these maxims is appropriate as a general rule of life; and the attempt to treat them as such has led to a regrettable amount of hypocrisy and moral confusion.

Eternal Punishment

The most intolerable of the doctrines taught by Jesus, and the one that has had the most hideous social consequences, is the doctrine of hell. This doctrine is still accepted and taught by the Catholic Church, but Christians of other denominations are making desperate attempts to explain it away. But Jesus' statements on the subject are so frequent, and so explicit, that if they are to be dismissed as symbolic or unhistorical it becomes hard to see why any of his reported sayings should be accepted as literally true.

One fortunate result of the decline in Bible-reading is that few people today are entirely familiar with Jesus' statements about hell, so it will be my unpleasant duty to quote some of the more horrific of them.

> The Son of man shall send forth his angels, and they shall gather out of his Kingdom all things that offend, and them which do iniquity; and shall cast them into a furnace of fire: there shall be wailing and gnashing of teeth. (Matt. xiii, 41–42)
>
> Then shall he say also unto them on the left hand, Depart from me ye cursed, into everlasting fire, prepared for the devil and his angels. . . . And these shall go away into everlasting punishment. (Matt. xxv, 41, 46)
>
> Be not afraid of them that kill the body, and after that have no more that they can do. . . . But . . . fear him, which after he hath killed hath power to cast into hell; yea, I say unto you, Fear him. (Luke xii, 4, 5)
>
> He that shall blaspheme against the Holy Ghost hath never forgiveness, but is in danger of eternal damnation. (Mark iii, 29)
>
> Whosoever shall say [to his brother] Thou fool, shall be in danger of hell fire. (Matt. v, 22)
>
> If thy hand offend thee, cut it off: it is better for thee to enter into life maimed, than having two hands to go into hell, into the fire that never shall be quenched. (Mark ix, 43)
>
> Wide is the gate, and broad is the way, that leadeth to destruction, and many there be which go in thereat. (Matt. xii, 13)

We have also the parable of Dives and Lazarus (Luke xvi, 19–31), in which Dives is consigned to everlasting torment for no greater crime than that he was wealthy and carefree, and took insufficient thought for the beggar at his gate. The story relates how Dives, tormented with pain and thirst, begged unavailingly for a drop of water; and when, more magnanimous than his torturers, he asked that his brothers on earth might be warned 'lest they, too, come unto this place of torment' he received only the curt answer 'they have Moses and the prophets; let them hear them'. It is hard to see why this tale should be regarded as edifying.

I have in my possession a newspaper cutting which describes how a father punished his six-year-old son for stealing by holding his hand over a gas jet. His behaviour was described as 'inhuman' and 'barbaric' and he was imprisoned for three months. Jesus' teaching suggests that different standards apply to our Heavenly Father, who, though by definition all-good and all-loving, will inflict hideous torments throughout eternity on those who displease him, for no motive but vengeance—since there is no possibility of repentance and redemption in hell. The inconsistency is so gross that it amply justifies the description of Christianity as a schizophrenic religion.

The doctrine of hell was not entirely of Jesus' invention. Though belief in a future life was quite foreign to most Old Testament writers, it had begun to creep into Jewish thought around the second century BC, and the idea of posthumous suffering for the wicked was foreshadowed by one of the latest of the Old Testament writers, Daniel ('Many of them that sleep in the dust of the earth shall awake, some to everlasting life, some to shame and everlasting contempt' xii, 2). But the doctrine

4

of everlasting torment was no part of official Jewish teaching, so there is no obvious reason why Jesus should have embraced it with such enthusiasm. What case can be made for the view, propounded uneasily by present-day Protestants, that his statements were not meant to be taken literally?

It can be argued that the fire, at least, must be metaphorical, since in a literal fire the bodies of the damned would be consumed (though some theologians, including Augustine, have suggested that the resurrected body may be made of non-combustible material). But there is no need to pursue these subtleties, since even if the fire is metaphorical, it is a metaphor intended to convey the extremity of agony; and a God who consigns anyone, however wicked, to an eternity of agony is a sadistic monster who deserves execration rather than love.

The most generally accepted view among Protestants today is that hell-fire is a symbolic expression designed to convey the agony of the soul's separation from God. It is commonly added that the souls in hell, by rejecting God, have freely chosen their own destiny, so that God, who has given them free will, would be breaking his pledge if he were to prevent the full consequences of their choice. But this is mere sophistry. If separation from God were in itself agonizing, then clearly no-one would choose it. And if, as the Gospels repeatedly say, the agony is inflicted as a punishment for rejecting God, then, though the victims may have willed the rejection, there is no reason to suppose that they willed the consequences. Shorn of the pious language, the Protestant interpretation differs little from the Communist argument that those who choose to oppose the regime bring their fate on themselves.

Moreover, attempts to explain away hell as 'symbolic' involve a difficulty that few Christians have faced. If Jesus' statements about hell were not meant to be taken literally, why, it may be asked, did he make them in a form that ensured that they *would* be taken literally—as they have been throughout most of the Christian era? They have probably caused more terror and misery, more cruelty and more violation of natural human sympathy, than any religious teaching in the history of mankind. Was this what Jesus intended? Or did he misjudge the effect of his words? Either view is difficult to reconcile with the belief that he was God.

Anti-intellectualism

Jesus and Socrates are sometimes classed together as two of the great moral teachers of history, who were put to death because their message was too advanced for the authorities of their time. But it would be hard to find two teachers whose aims were more sharply contrasted.

Socrates addressed himself primarily to intelligent young men, to whom he gave every encouragement to think for themselves. Jesus' chosen disciples were unlettered peasants from whom he demanded uncritical belief and unquestioning obedience. Willingness to accept beliefs on authority and without evidence was for Socrates an intellectual crime; for Jesus it was the first of virtues. Socrates encouraged his young followers to develop towards maturity; Jesus tried to reduce his to the level of children. The Gospels contain numerous statements in which the attitudes of children are compared favourably with those of adults. For example: 'Except ye be converted, and become as little children, ye shall not enter into the Kingdom of heaven' (Matt. xviii, 3). 'I thank thee, O Father, . . . that thou hast hid these things from the wise and prudent, and hast revealed them unto babes' (Luke x, 21). These statements are so often quoted with approval that probably few pause to consider whether it is really a good thing for adults to think and behave like children.

What attracted Jesus towards 'little children', obviously, was their unquestioning trust in adults, and his ideal was to be surrounded by adults who had a similar trust in him. Such trust was not readily obtainable from educated Jews, who showed a troublesome tendency to ask for evidence for his Messianic claims—requests which Jesus angrily refused to satisfy. 'A wicked and adulterous generation seeketh after a sign; and there shall no sign be given unto it' (Matt. xvi, 4).

Jesus' distrust of intelligence and education was shared by Paul, who wrote 'If any man among you seemeth to be wise in this world, let him become a fool that he may be wise. For the wisdom of this world is foolishness with God. For it is written . . . The Lord knoweth the thoughts of the wise, that they are vain' (I Cor. iii, 18–21).

The same attitude persisted among the early Christians, as can be illustrated from Celsus' *The True Doctrine*,* which dates from the second century AD. Celsus wrote:

Christians usually flee headlong from cultured people,

* This book, like most other pagan writings that were unfavourable to Christianity, was destroyed when the Roman Empire became Christian. But parts of it were preserved in *Contra Celsum*, in which Origen, one of the Greek fathers of the Church, quoted and paraphrased Celsus' arguments at length as a preliminary to attacking them.

who are not prepared to be deceived; but they trap illiterate folk. . . . Their injunctions are like this. 'Let no one educated, no one wise, no one sensible draw near. For these abilities are thought by us to be evils. But as for anyone ignorant, anyone stupid, anyone uneducated, anyone who is a child, let him come boldly.' . . . Some of them do not even want to give or receive a reason for what they believe, and use such expressions as 'Do not ask questions; just believe', and 'Thy faith will save thee'. And they say, 'The wisdom in the world is an evil, and foolishness a good thing'. . . . But why is it bad to have been educated and to have studied the best doctrines, and both to be and to appear intelligent?[9]

Celsus' question received no answer, and in the centuries that followed the Church continued to extol credulity and to fear and distrust the free intelligence—with results that will be considered in Part II.

Sex and Marriage

Jesus was unmarried—a condition so rare among Jews at that time that the language did not contain a word for 'bachelor'. The only celibates were the members of ascetic communities such as the Essenes, a fact which lends support to the suggestion that Jesus may have spent his early years in an Essene monastery.

His attitude to sexual love was consistent with his attitude to family affection and family ties in general—that his followers should avoid them as far as possible, since they tended to interfere with an exclusive devotion to God. Thus he spoke with apparent approval of those who have 'made themselves eunuchs for the kingdom of

heaven's sake' (Matt. xix, 12),* and assured his disciples
that there would be no marriage in the world to come
('They which shall be accounted worthy to obtain that
world, and the resurrection from the dead, neither marry
nor are given in marriage' (Luke xx, 35)).

However, he does not seem to have been a misogynist.
He is represented as having a natural and friendly relationship with the Bethany sisters, Martha and Mary; he
attended a wedding at Cana, where the miracle he is said
to have performed would doubtless have added greatly to
the success of the occasion; and the incident of the woman
taken in adultery shows him at his most attractive ('He
that is without sin among you, let him first cast a stone at
her,' John viii, 7). In general his attitude towards sex and
marriage seems to reflect lack of interest rather than active
disapproval—in contrast with Paul, who was preoccupied
with the need to 'keep under [the] body and bring it into
subjection' (I Cor. ix, 27), and who wrote to the Corin-
thians: 'It is good for a man not to touch a woman. . . .
But if they cannot contain, let them marry: for it
is better to marry than to burn [i.e. with passion]' (I
Cor. vii, 1, 9).

Injunctions of this kind resounded with disastrous
effect throughout the Dark and Middle Ages, and their

* There is room for argument about whether this statement was
meant literally, as Origen and others supposed, or whether it was
merely a dramatic way of saying 'have lived as celibates'. The trans-
lators of the New English Bible adopt the second view; and, allowing
their opinion about what Jesus 'really meant' to influence—some
would say unduly—their rendering of what he said, have translated
eunouchisan eautous as 'have renounced marriage'. But this interpretation becomes very forced when it is applied to the first part of the
sentence, which, literally translated, runs 'For there are some eunuchs
who were so born from their mothers' womb, and some eunuchs who
were made eunuchs by men'.

echoes are still audible in the Catholic Church. But it is fair to say that nothing said either by Jesus or by Paul justifies the pathological sex-hatred of the Early Fathers—a matter which will be discussed more fully in Chapter 16.

PART II

CHRISTIANITY IN HISTORY

INTRODUCTION

Many Christians today take up a somewhat paradoxical attitude. They claim that Christianity is the source of all that is best in our culture, while admitting nevertheless that Christianity's historical record is in many respects appalling. They usually try to resolve the paradox by making a distinction between 'true Christianity'—the teaching of the Gospels—and 'the Church' which has misunderstood and distorted this teaching. It is true Christianity, they claim, that abolished gladiatorial shows, kept learning alive after the fall of Rome, improved the position of women, and brought about the abolition of slavery. It is the Church that is responsible for Christianity's intolerance and obscurantism, the torrents of blood shed in its crusades and sectarian quarrels, its atrocious cruelty towards unbelievers and heretics, its witch-hunting and anti-Semitism, and its neurotic attitude towards sex.

The claims made for 'true Christianity' will be considered later. My present concern is to suggest that most of the evils laid at the door of 'the Church' are the result, not of misinterpreting Gospel teaching, but of taking it to its logical conclusion.

THE EFFECTS OF BELIEF IN HELL

Most of the worst evils for which Christianity was responsible spring directly or indirectly from the terrible doctrine of hell.

It has already been argued (pp. 40–1) that no convincing case can be made for saying that Jesus' statements on this subject were not meant to be taken literally. They were certainly taken literally by the early Church. Thus Paul wrote of Jesus at the second coming 'in flaming fire taking vengeance on them that know not God and that obey not the Gospel of our Lord Jesus Christ: who shall be punished with everlasting destruction' (II Thess i, 8–9). And the author of the book of Revelation, dating from the first century AD, wrote exultantly of the torments that awaited the wicked—embellishing the Gospel accounts, which one would have thought were sufficiently lurid, with additional touches of his own, such as 'the lake which burneth with fire and brimstone' (xx, 8). And the concluding verses of Mark (xvi, 9–20), which are now regarded by biblical scholars as a late addition, contain the sentence 'He that believeth and is baptised, shall be saved; but he that believeth not shall be damned'—which indicates the state of opinion in the second century AD, from which the addition is said to date.

Life in the Dark Ages was overshadowed by the terror of hell. It led many believers, such as St Jerome (cf. pp. 71–2) to withdraw completely from the world and subject themselves for years on end to a solitary regime of starvation and self-torture, in the hope of avoiding a still worse fate in the life to come. In the Middle Ages, when the Church's stranglehold on the human mind began to weaken and certain heretical ideas gained currency, it was held, not illogically, that any degree of cruelty towards heretics was justified if there was a chance that it could save them, or others, from the eternal torments of hell. Thus, during some seven centuries, in the name of the religion of love, hundreds of thousands of people were not merely killed but atrociously tortured in ways that make the gas chambers of Belsen seem humane.

Belief in hell made death terrifying to the Christian. Some of the Early Fathers, it is true, clearly felt that their own sanctity was sufficient to remove them from danger, and among these St Thomas Aquinas, Peter Lombard and others explained to the faithful that 'In order that the happiness of the Saints may be more delightful, and that they may render more copious thanks to God for it, they are allowed to see perfectly the sufferings of the damned.'[1] But to those less confident of their own final destiny the dread of hell must have been ever-present. At the Renaissance the spread of scepticism, represented by such writers as Montaigne, probably reduced the fear of damnation among the educated. But the Reformation set things back again. Luther was a firm believer in hell-fire, and the following quotation from his *Table Talk* highlights the sad contrast between the serene resignation with which the best of the pagans faced death, and the terrors of the Christian.

It were a light and an easy matter for a Christian to suffer and overcome death if he knew not that it were

God's wrath; the same title maketh death bitter to us. But an heathen dieth securely away; he neither seeth nor feeleth that it is God's wrath, but meaneth it is the end of nature and is natural. The epicurean says it is but to endure one evil hour.[2]

Bunyan, born a century and a half after Luther, described his own childhood terrors of hell in a book entitled without deliberate irony *Grace Abounding to the Chief of Sinners*:

> I was [in my childhood] greatly afflicted and troubled with the thoughts of the day of judgment, and that both night and day, and would tremble at the thoughts of the fearful torments of hell fire; still fearing that it would be my lot to be found at last amongst those devils and hellish fiends, who are there bound down with the chains and bonds of eternal darkness. . . .
>
> These things, I say, when I was but a child but nine or ten years old, did so distress my soul, that when in the midst of my many sports and childish vanities, amidst my vain companions, I was often much cast down and afflicted in my mind therewith, yet could I not let go my sins. Yea, I was also then so overcome with despair of life and heaven, that I should often wish either that there had been no hell, or that I had been a devil—supposing they were only tormentors; that if it must needs be that I went thither, I might be rather a tormentor, than be tormented myself.

Bunyan later came to believe that his sins were forgiven. But other great writers never reached this consoling conviction. Johnson, as Boswell relates, was haunted throughout his life by the terror of death and damnation. The poet Cowper became convinced that he had committed

the sin against the Holy Ghost and was destined for hell—
a conviction which exacerbated a pre-existing tendency
to melancholia to the point of recurrent insanity. His
biographer, Maurice Quinlan, relates how on his deathbed 'the clergyman proceeded to speak of the merciful
Redeemer who loved his children and would welcome
him to a state of infinite happiness. These words, however, provoked an anguished cry from Cowper, and he
begged Johnson not to mention again the subject of an
after life.'[3]

Thousands of unrecorded lives must have been ruined
by similar terrors. A few Protestants may have found
reassurance when in 1864 the Privy Council 'dismissed
hell with costs' (as an ironic commentator put it), by
upholding the appeal against dismissal of an Anglican
clergyman who had denied that it was 'an essential
doctrine of the Church of England that wicked men are
irretrievably damned and will be punished for ever'. But
the effects of this decision are unlikely to have percolated
very far. Sir Osbert Sitwell in his autobiography describes
himself as suffering the familiar childish agonies around
the turn of the century.

> My nights, occupied with my private problem . . .
> nights filled with my picturings of hell flames, my
> efforts to overcome my terror of them, or to think,
> equally, of some way of avoiding them through virtue,
> became an absolute torment . . . I now betrayed symp-
> toms of an intense neurasthenia. . . . After all, if the
> Christian religion was true, then hell existed; and if hell
> existed, as it was so elaborately and even exultantly
> described in various passages in the Bible, and if I was
> as wicked as I was frequently told I was by my mentors,
> then I ought to take the whole matter with the utmost

seriousness. . . . Yet none of those round me—except my aunt Florence—seemed to be excessively worried about it. Alas, the more I thought of it, the worse became the torments of my nights, and the worse, in consequence, my conduct, willy-nilly, the following day.[4]

Few children, it may be hoped, suffer similar anguish today. But in so far as this is so, it is not, as is often claimed, because present-day Christianity has attained a deeper understanding of the true meaning of the Gospel message. It is rather because present-day Christianity is progressively rejecting the more intolerable parts of the Gospel message. But by 'Christianity' here must be understood Protestant Christianity. The Catholic Church still teaches the doctrine of eternal punishment, and some of its recent pronouncements on the subject will be quoted in Chapter 19.

SEVEN

THE PERSECUTION OF THE CHRISTIANS
AND THE CONVERSION OF ROME

So many misconceptions prevail about the early Christians and their treatment by the Roman authorities that a brief historical outline is necessary to put the facts in perspective.

At the time of the birth of Jesus, there prevailed in Rome a degree of religious tolerance almost unparalleled in history. The state religion was still the worship of the gods of Olympus, supplemented since the time of Augustus by worship of the Emperor as a divinity. Educated Romans observed the formalities of the official religion, though without taking it very seriously. Most of them—or at all events most of those whose writings have come down to us—gave their main adherence to one or other of the great schools of Humanist philosophy, Stoicism or Epicureanism, that derived from Greece. But the ordinary population required something more superstitious and colourful, and for many of them this need was amply provided by the various 'mystery religions'. These were somewhat esoteric cults, mostly deriving from the East, which, unlike Stoicism and Epicureanism, promised eternal life to their adherents, and which had a common element of 'mystery', in the sense of secret rites and ceremonies to which only initiates were admitted.

Adherence to one of these cults in no way implied rejection of the state religion. The idea of exclusive devotion to one god, or to one hierarchy of gods, was quite foreign to the Romans, and the state was completely tolerant of the mystery cults so long as their adherents respected the official religion and made the formal gesture of sprinkling a pinch of incense on the altars of the gods on state occasions—an action which was patriotic rather than religious, and was probably roughly equivalent to our own practice of standing up when *God Save the Queen* is played.

Among the most important of the mystery religions were Mithraism, the Eleusinian mysteries, and the worship of Isis and Osiris—the last of which originated in Egypt in about 4000 BC and survived in the West until well after the conversion of Rome. It is unlikely that Christianity's life-span will prove as long.

By most Romans at the beginning of the Christian era, Christianity was regarded as just another mystery religion. There was, however, one important difference. The mystery religions, as already stated, were nothing if not tolerant. There was no objection to a person's being initiated into more than one of them, and initiates felt no difficulty about making the routine respectful gestures towards the state religion. But the Christians refused to burn incense on the pagan altars. They demanded exclusive devotion to one God, and declared that all who did not worship this God would be condemned to eternal torment. It was probably this last threat that most outraged the Romans, and led those of them that knew anything of Christianity to describe its adherents as 'haters of mankind'.

And there were other factors that made the Christians disliked. Not only did they refuse to burn incense to the pagan gods; they sometimes denounced and insulted these gods and even defaced their shrines. They avoided civic duties and refused to serve in the army. Their doctrine that the poor and the humble would inherit the earth led to the suspicion that they were fomenting social revolution; and their communion ceremonies exposed them, not unnaturally, to the imputation of cannibalism.

It is not surprising that the Christians were unpopular, but until the reign of Nero they endured nothing worse than unpopularity. Then, however, in the year 64 AD, a large part of Rome was destroyed by a fire of unknown origin, and the Emperor, who was probably insane, was suspected of being responsible. To divert this suspicion he laid the blame on the Christians, and subjected them to abominable cruelties which have been described by the Roman historian, Tacitus. He wrote:

To crush the rumour therefore Nero provided as culprits, and punished with every form of severity, persons who were hated for their abominations and generally known as Christians. This name had originated with one Christus, who had been put to death by the procurator Pontius Pilate in the reign of Tiberius. The pernicious superstition had been suppressed for a time; but was breaking out again, not only in Judaea, where the trouble had started, but even in the City, where everything foul and shameful from any source collects and finds a following. Self-confessed Christians were arrested first; then on their evidence vast numbers were convicted, not on charges arising from the fire, but for hatred of mankind. As they died they also provided sport, by being wrapped in the skins of wild animals and torn to death by dogs, or by being fastened to crosses so that, when daylight was past, their burning gave light by night. Nero had offered his own garden for this show; and provided a performance at the

circus, either mixing with the crowd himself, dressed
as a driver, or standing in his own chariot. As a result
these men, though their wickedness deserved exemplary
punishment, aroused sympathy since their death was
occasioned, not by needs of state, but to satisfy the
savagery of a single individual.[1]

This account was written nearly fifty years after the
event, and is probably coloured by hindsight—it is
unlikely that many Romans at the time of Nero felt the
contempt and detestation for Christianity that Tacitus
shows.

Today, over one of the entrances to the Colosseum in
Rome, is placed a large wooden cross in commemoration
of the Christians who died there. And many tourists must
gaze at it with emotion as they visualize Nero's helpless
victims being torn and mangled by wild beasts. But in
fact the Colosseum did not exist in the time of Nero—its
construction was begun in the reign of his successor,
Vespasian—and there is no real evidence that any Christians met their death there, except as gladiators. Few,
indeed, suffered for their faith anywhere in Rome after
the death of Nero, since from that time onward persecution was largely confined to the provinces.

Nero died in AD 68, and for the next twenty-seven
years the Church was left in peace. In AD 95, however,
there was a brief outbreak of persecution in the reign of
Domitian, a tyrannical despot who also persecuted the
Stoics. The persecution was not very severe however, and
on the death of Domitian, according to the Christian
writer Lactantius:

The acts of the tyrant being revoked, the Church was
not only restored to its former state, but shone forth

with a greater splendour and luxuriance; and a period
following in which many good sovereigns wielded the
Imperial sceptre, it suffered no assaults from its enemies
but stretched out its hands to the east and to the west
... but at last the long peace was broken. After many
years, that hateful monster Decius arose, who troubled
the Church.[2]

This picture is somewhat too favourable, since out-
breaks of persecution undoubtedly did occur in the
provinces in the period referred to. But such acts were
localized and sporadic, and usually originated with the
populace rather than with the authorities. When un-
expected misfortunes such as famine or epidemics
occurred the people, not unnaturally, were inclined to
attribute them either to the evil machinations of the
Christian deity or to the anger of the pagan gods whom
the Christians had insulted; and it was sometimes difficult
for the Roman governor to resist their demand for
vengeance.

A famous exchange of letters between Pliny the
younger and the Emperor Trajan throws some light on
the official attitude at this time. Pliny was governor of
Bithynia, a province in Asia Minor, and in AD 112 he
wrote to the Emperor for guidance in the treatment of
Christians, whose 'infectious superstition', as he put it,
was becoming widespread and creating a problem. He
wished particularly to know whether 'nominal Christianity without crime deserves punishment, or only when
crime is coupled with it'.[3] The Emperor's reply was brief
and may be quoted in full.

My dear Pliny, you have adopted the right method in
examining the cases of the Christians who were brought

before you. For there can be no general rule which could establish a fixed procedure. There should be no search made for Christians; though, if they are summoned and convicted, they must be punished. But the method should be that anyone who denies that he is a Christian and proves it by his actions, namely by worshipping our gods, whatever suspicion he may previously have incurred, should earn pardon by repentance. Public accusations by anonymous persons should have no place in criminal practice. Such a procedure would be thoroughly bad and out of keeping with the spirit of our age.[3]

Towards the middle of the third century opposition to Christianity took a more political form, as barbarian pressure increased the need for unity. In the year 249, in the reign of Decius, there was issued for the first time an official edict against Christianity which aimed at extirpating the religion throughout the empire. It was followed by an outbreak of ferocity which lasted until the death of Decius two years later. Thereafter there was comparative and uneasy calm until 303 when an edict of Diocletian set on foot the most savage and prolonged persecution which the Church had to endure. Christian churches were ordered to be destroyed, Christians were deprived of all civil rights, and assembly for worship was made punishable with death. Later, Christians were ordered to sacrifice to the gods under pain of torture.

The centre of the persecution was Nicomedia, in Asia Minor, where Diocletian's palace was situated;* and

---

* By the time of Diocletian, the empire was not governed by a single ruler, but by two emperors known as Augusti and two subordinate colleagues known as Caesars. Diocletian was Augustus of the eastern part of the empire.

Gibbon relates how, when the first edict was exhibited there, it was at once torn down by a Christian 'who expressed at the same time, by the bitterest invectives, his contempt as well as abhorrence for such impious and tyrannical governors. . . . He was burnt, or rather roasted, by a slow fire; and his executioners, zealous to revenge the personal insult which had been offered to the emperors, exhausted every refinement of cruelty, without being able to subdue his patience, or to alter the steady and insulting smile which, in his dying agonies, he still preserved in his countenance.'[4]

In the years that followed, many hundreds must have met equally horrible deaths, and faced them with equal fortitude—a fortitude strengthened by the conviction that those who died as martyrs were certain of heaven, and that once their agonies were over they would enter immediately into everlasting bliss. So strong was this conviction that many Christians not only faced martyrdom but actively sought it. Even before the persecution of Diocletian the desire for martyrdom had become at times so widespread that the Church had to exert her authority to prevent her followers from thrusting themselves into the hands of the persecutors. Tertullian[5] relates how in a small Asiatic town the entire population once flocked to the proconsul declaring themselves Christians and inviting him to put them to death. 'That bewildered functionary' (in Lecky's appealing phrase) asked them whether, if they were so weary of life, there were no precipices or ropes with which they could end their days. But this, of course, would not have satisfied the requirements of martyrdom, so eventually the official compromised by putting a few of the suppliants to death and dismissing the others.

It was probably this ardour for martyrdom that provoked Marcus Aurelius to his only explicit reference to the Christians. He wrote:

> The soul should be ready, when the hour of release from the body comes, to be extinguished or to be scattered or to survive. But such readiness should proceed from inward conviction, and not come of mere perversity, as with the Christians: it should result from a temper rational and grave, and—if it is to convince others—is should be unostentatious.[6]

In 305 Diocletian abdicated, and was succeeded by the far more implacable Galerius, who continued the persecution relentlessly for six more years. No-one knows how many Christians died during this period. Wildly extravagant claims have been made by Christian historians, but Gibbon, estimating and extrapolating freely on the basis of the small amount of reliable information available, has concluded that the number who died for their faith during the persecutions of Diocletian and Galerius was probably around two thousand—a total which sinks almost into insignificance beside the number of Christians killed in doctrinal disputes with their fellow-Christians in the ages of faith.

In 311 Galerius was struck down by a revolting disease which was probably cancer of the bowels. He apparently attributed the disease to the vengeance of the Christian God, and before his death he issued a proclamation restoring civil liberties to the Christians, permitting them to rebuild their churches, and asking their prayers for his recovery. He was succeeded by Constantine I, who was converted to Christianity in 312, apparently as the result of witnessing an unusual meteorological phenomenon which he interpreted as a sign from heaven;[7] and under Constantine Christianity became the official religion of the Roman Empire.

EIGHT

SECTARIAN STRIFE

By the time of Constantine's accession, the Empire had been seriously weakened. To defend it against barbarians from Central Asia Rome had had increasingly to withdraw troops from the western provinces, until the territory she effectively controlled was reduced to the countries around the eastern Mediterranean. Geographically, Rome was no longer the centre of the Empire, and in 330 Constantine transferred the capital to the site of the ancient Greek city of Byzantium, on the Bosphorus. There he built a magnificent city named after him, Constantinople, which for eleven centuries remained the centre of eastern Christendom.

Constantinople, known as 'the second Rome' became a beautiful and civilized city with a university and a magnificent cathedral. But in the Byzantine or Eastern★ Empire of which it was the capital, civilization was less in evidence. It might have been expected that once the threat of pagan persecution was reduced, Christians would live together in brotherly harmony. But in the event they proved far more intolerant than their Roman persecutors, and in the centuries that followed the foundation of Constantinople, parts of the Eastern Empire were

★ The term 'Eastern' was at first something of a misnomer, as the empire originally extended as far west as North Africa. But in the next four centuries its boundaries contracted steadily towards the east as a result of Arab pressure.

repeatedly drenched in blood from the warfare of Christian with Christian.

From the first, the Christian Church had shown a tendency to divide into sects. Before the conversion of Constantine, there had been a major split between the Alexandrians (the orthodox party) who held that 'the Son coexists ingenerately with God . . . neither in thought nor by a single moment does God precede the Son'[1] and the Arians, who held that the Son 'came into being by God's will and council . . . and before He was begotten or created or determined or founded, He did not exist'.[1] It was largely in the hope of resolving this and other disputes that Constantine called the first council of the entire Christian world at Nicaea in 325—a year which was a landmark in Christian history. This Council produced the Nicene creed, which favoured the orthodox doctrine. But sects continued to proliferate, and at the beginning of the fifth century Augustine estimated their number as at least eighty-eight.

The issues which divided the sects now seem unbelievably trivial. There were the Homoousians (the orthodox party) who held that the Son and the Father were of one and the same essence, as opposed to the Homoiousians or semi-Arians who held that their essences were separate though exactly similar. There were the Monophysites, who held that Christ united two natures, the divine and the human, in person, and the Nestorians, who held that he possessed two distinct personalities.* These subtle distinctions might be thought ideal material for academic debate. But to the early Christians they were the occasion for bloodshed.

---

* This controversy lasted for centuries, and was taken with great seriousness by Cardinal Newman. Cf. *Apologia pro Vita Sua*, part V.

It is in this context particularly that the claim is made that the misdeeds of the Church represent a perversion of true Christianity. And it is true that there is nothing in the Gospels to justify, or even account for, the hair-splitting sectarianism that bedevilled the early Church. But it was Jesus' teaching about hell, and the paramount importance of true belief, that explained the savagery with which the sects persecuted one another. To quote Lecky:

> If we consider the actual history of the Church since Constantine, we shall find no justification for the popular theory that beneath its influence the narrow spirit of patriotism faded into a wide and cosmopolitan philanthropy. A real though somewhat languid feeling of universal brotherhood had already been created in the world by the universality of the Roman Empire. In the new faith the range of genuine sympathy was strictly limited by the creed. According to the popular belief, all who differed from the teaching of the orthodox lived under the hatred of the Almighty, and were destined after death for an eternity of anguish. . . . The eighty or ninety sects, into which Christianity speedily divided, hated one another with an intensity that extorted the wonder of Julian and the ridicule of the pagans of Alexandria, and the fierce riots and persecutions that hatred produced appeared in every page of ecclesiastical history. . . . The Donatists, having separated from the orthodox simply on the question of the validity of the consecration of a certain bishop, declared that all who adopted the orthodox view must be damned, refused to perform their rites in the orthodox churches which they had seized till they had burnt the altar and scraped the wood, beat multitudes to death with clubs, blinded others by anointing their eyes with

lime, filled Africa, during nearly two centuries, with war and desolation, and contributed largely to its final ruin. The childish and almost unintelligible quarrels between the Homoiousians and the Homoousians . . . filled the world with riot and hatred. The Catholics tell . . . how three thousand persons perished in the riots that convulsed Constantinople when the Arian Bishop Macedonius superseded the Athanasian Paul. . . . In Ephesus, during the contest between St Cyril and the Nestorians, the cathedral itself was the theatre of a fierce and bloody conflict. . . . Later, when the Monophysite controversy was at its height, the palace of the emperor at Constantinople was blockaded, the churches were besieged, and the streets commanded by furious bands of contending monks . . .[2]

Furthermore, Lecky continued, there arose at this time

. . . a literature surpassing in its mendacious ferocity any other the world had known. The polemical writers habitually painted as daemons those who diverged from the orthodox belief, gloated with a vindictive piety over the sufferings of the heretic upon earth, as upon a Divine punishment, and . . . exulted in no ambiguous terms on the tortures which they believed to be reserved for him [beyond the grave]. He who will compare the beautiful pictures the Greek poets gave of their Trojan adversaries, or the Roman historians of the enemies of their country, with those which ecclesiastical writers, for many centuries, almost invariably gave of all who were opposed to their Church, may easily estimate the extent to which cosmopolitan sympathy had retrograded.[2]

Those who hold that the world was redeemed by the coming of Christianity would find it hard to point to many signs of redemption at this period of history.

NINE

THE DARK AGES AND THE CULT OF ASCETICISM

The history of the Western Empire, still centred in Rome, followed a different course. In the fourth and fifth centuries it was swept by successive waves of barbarian invaders, who set up kingdoms in various parts of Europe and eventually broke the power of Rome itself. Rome was sacked by the Goths in 410 and by the Vandals in 455; and in 476 the last Roman emperor was deposed, and was succeeded by the Goth, Odoacer, who ruled nominally as the vice-regent of the Emperor of the East.

In the centuries that followed the division of the Empire and the fall of Rome—a period commonly known as the Dark Ages—European civilization sank to its lowest ebb. Almost the whole of western Europe was illiterate; even the Emperor Charlemagne, though he had mastered the art of reading, was unable to write, and with few exceptions the skills of reading and writing were confined to the monasteries and to the Jews.*

However, western Europe in the Dark Ages was at

---

* The achievements of the Jews in education have not been sufficiently recognized. From the beginning of the Christian era they held their communities together by systematic education, and later, to quote Cecil Roth 'At a period when the vast majority of Europeans were illiterate, the Jews insisted as a religious duty upon a system of universal education of remarkable comprehensiveness' (*A Short History of the Jewish People*, 1935, pp. 219-20).

least free from the sectarian quarrels and the warfare of Christian with Christian that ravaged the East. In 390, before the sack of Rome, the emperor Theodosius had had all pagan temples razed to the ground, and had prohibited pagan worship throughout the Empire; and by the time of the barbarian conquests Roman paganism had died down to a flicker.

The invading Goths and Vandals sat lightly to their own primitive religion of nature-worship, and made no attempt to impose it on the peoples they had conquered. On the contrary, they themselves embraced Christianity— though it was a Christianity that embodied many elements, only superficially Christianized, of their own nature-religion. In Rome, conversion seems to have been complete within a generation; and though 'heathen' beliefs and practices survived for some centuries in outlying provinces such as Saxony, these areas were conquered and forcibly re-Christianized in the eighth century by Charlemagne, King of the Franks.

Charlemagne is almost the only figure to emerge with any clarity from the mists of the Dark Ages. He was a powerful ruler and a man of great ability, and in 800 he was crowned in Rome by the Pope and proclaimed ruler, not only of his own Frankish Kingdom, but of all the provinces of western Europe that had embraced Christianity—an assemblage that came later to be known as the Holy Roman Empire. The strong rule of Charlemagne succeeded for a time in restoring to western Christendom something of the unity that had obtained in the pagan Empire, and during his lifetime the Emperor and the Pope—the temporal and spiritual monarchs—reigned as co-equals. But Charlemagne had no worthy successor, and after his death the Empire fell apart, and the Church resumed her former status as the dominant power in Europe—a status which she retained until the Renaissance.

Asceticism

The beginning of the Dark Ages witnessed one of the strangest phenomena in Christian history—the cult of asceticism which persisted for some two centuries after the fall of Rome. During this period, western Christianity put fervently into practice nearly all the most unattractive features of Jesus' teaching. It regarded human ties and affections as an obstacle to the love of God, and though it proclaimed the duty of charity it taught that we should do good to others, not from affection or spontaneous impulse, but because this was what God commanded and what God would reward. And the last people we should do good to were the members of our own family.

This doctrine was widely expressed and practised by the Early Fathers, one of whom, St Jerome (fourth-fifth century), may be quoted. (Jerome was responsible for the first Latin translation of the Bible, known as the Vulgate, and is one of the most highly-esteemed saints in the Christian calendar.) His ideal of feminine excellence was embodied in one Paula, a patrician Roman lady, a widow with five children, who on her husband's death devoted herself to the ascetic life and became the head of a convent. Jerome wrote of her:

> How can I describe her far-reaching kindness even to those whom she had never seen? . . . What bedridden person was not supported with money from her purse? She would seek out such with the greatest diligence . . . and would think it her loss were any hungry or sick person to be supported by another's food. She robbed

her children; and, when her relatives remonstrated with her for doing so, she declared that she was leaving to them a better inheritance in the mercy of Christ.... 'God is my witness' she said 'that what I do I do for his sake. My prayer is that I may die a beggar, not leaving a penny to my daughter and indebted to strangers for my winding sheet.... She obtained her wish at last, and died leaving her daughter overwhelmed with a mass of debt ... and a crowd of brothers and sisters whom it is hard for her to support, but whom it would be undutiful to cast off. Could there be a more admirable instance of virtue?[1]

The phrase beginning 'and would think it her loss' is significant; it suggests that Paula was concerned less to relieve others' suffering than to enhance her own sanctity. This attitude was widespread in the Dark Ages. As Lecky remarked 'A form of what may be termed selfish charity arose.... Men gave money to the poor, simply and exclusively for their own spiritual benefit, and the welfare of the sufferer was altogether foreign to their thoughts'.[2] From this attitude it was but a short step to the view that self-sacrifice brings spiritual benefits for the sacrificer, even though it does nothing for the welfare of anyone else; and in the first centuries after the conversion of Europe, the great exemplars of Christian virtue were held to be the hermits—men who cut themselves off from all human relationships and lived alone in the desert or wilderness, starving and scourging themselves and (as they supposed) growing daily in holiness. Jerome spent some years of his life in this way and wrote an account from which the following is quoted:

Many years ago, for the sake of the Kingdom of

Heaven I cut myself off from home, parents, sister, relations, and, what was harder, from the dainty food to which I had been used. . . . But oh how often, when I was living in the desert, in that lonely waste, scorched by the burning sun, which affords to hermits a savage dwelling-place, how often did I fancy myself surrounded by the pleasures of Rome! My unkempt limbs were covered in shapeless sackcloth; my skin through neglect had become as rough and black as an Ethiopian's. Tears and groans were every day my portion; and if sleep ever overcame my resistance and fell upon my eyes, I bruised my restless bones against the naked earth. Of food and drink I will not speak. Hermits drink nothing but cold water even when they are sick, and for them it is sinful luxury to partake of cooked dishes. But though in my fear of hell I had condemned myself to this prison-house, where my only companions were scorpions and wild beasts, I often found myself surrounded by bands of dancing girls. Though my limbs were cold as ice my mind was burning with desire, and the fires of lust kept bubbling up before me when my flesh was as good as dead.[3]

Similar austerities were practised by thousands of persons of both sexes in the Dark Ages. Lecky gives an account, based on patristic literature, of the revolting excesses of self-maceration and bodily squalor in which the ascetics indulged, and concludes:

There is perhaps no phase in the moral history of mankind of a deeper or more painful interest than this ascetic epidemic. A hideous, sordid and emaciated maniac, without knowledge, without patriotism, without natural affection, passing his life in a long routine of useless and atrocious self-torture, and quailing before the ghastly phantoms of his delirious brain, had become the ideal of the nations which had known the writings of Plato and Cicero and the lives of Socrates and Cato. For about two centuries, the hideous maceration of the body was regarded as the highest proof of excellence.[4]

Becoming a hermit meant, inevitably, breaking all ties with one's nearest and dearest, and in a letter to a young friend, Heliodorus, Jerome urged him not to shrink from this sacrifice.

> Though your little nephew hang on your neck, though your mother with dishevelled hair and torn raiment show you the breasts that gave you suck, though your father fling himself upon the threshold, trample your father underfoot and go your way, fly with tearless eyes to the standard of the cross. In these matters to be cruel is a son's duty. . . . I too have passed through all this. . . . The love of Christ and the fear of hell easily break such bonds as these.[5]

There are many stories in patristic literature about the heroic virtue with which aspirants to sainthood trampled on their natural affections. I quote (again from Lecky) a story paraphrased from one Cassian, a contemporary of Jerome.

> A man named Mutius, accompanied by his only child, a little boy of eight years old, abandoned his possessions and demanded admission into a monastery. The monks received him but they proceeded to discipline his heart. 'He had already forgotten that he was rich; he must next be taught to forget that he was a father!' His child was separated from him, clothed in

dirty rags, subjected to every form of gross and wanton hardship, beaten, spurned and ill-treated. Day after day the father was compelled to look upon his boy wasting away with sorrow, his once happy countenance for ever stained with tears, distorted by sobs of anguish. But yet, says the admiring biographer, 'though he saw this day by day, such was his love for Christ, and for the virtue of obedience, that the father's heart was rigid and unmoved. He thought little of the tears of his child. He was anxious only for his own humility and perfection in virtue!' . . . Mutius afterwards rose to a high position among the ascetics, and he was justly regarded as having displayed in great perfection the temper of a saint.[6]

The epidemic of extreme asceticism lasted for some two hundred years. But the ideals behind it—the self-centred pursuit of individual virtue, and the feeling that the endurance of useless suffering is good for the soul, and pleasing to God—these have persisted, though fortunately in diminishing strength, right through the Christian era, as some historical examples will illustrate.

In the Middle Ages, as distinct from the Dark Ages, the life of a hermit became less fashionable, but there was still a strong feeling that self-maceration was one of the highest forms of virtue. When, in 1170, the murdered body of St Thomas of Canterbury was undressed in the cathedral crypt, it was found to be encased from the neck to the knees in haircloth. Dean Stanley gives a description of the scene, based on various contemporary accounts.

The haircloth encased the whole body down to the knees; the hair drawers, as well as the rest of the dress, being covered on the outside with white linen so as to escape observation; and the whole so fastened together as to admit of being readily taken off for his daily scourgings, of which yesterday's portion was still apparent in the stripes on his body. Such austerity had hitherto been unknown to English saints, and the marvel was increased by the sight of the innumerable vermin with which the haircloth abounded—boiling over with them, as one account describes it, like water in a simmering cauldron. At the dreadful sight all the enthusiasm of the previous night revived with double ardour. They looked at each other in silent wonder; then exclaimed, 'See, see what a true monk he was, and we knew it not'; and burst into alternate fits of weeping and laughter, between the sorrow of having lost such a head, and the joy of having found such a saint.[7]

Moving on from the twelfth to the fourteenth century: the blessed Henry Suso, a German Dominican mystic, wrote (in the third person) an autobiography *The Life of the Servant* in which he described the almost incredible regime of self-torment to which he subjected himself for some sixteen years. To quote:

He was in his youth of a temperament full of fire and life; and when this began to make itself felt, it was very grievous to him; and he sought by many devices how he might bring his body into subjection. . . . He secretly caused an undergarment to be made for him; and in the undergarment he had strips of leather fixed, into which a hundred and fifty brass nails pointed and filed sharp, were driven, and the points of the nails were always turned towards the flesh. He had this garment made very tight, and so arranged as to go round him and fasten in front, in order that it might fit the closer to his body, and the pointed nails might be driven into his flesh; and it was high enough to reach upwards to his navel. In this he used to sleep at night. . . . The nights in winter were never so long, nor was the summer so hot, as to make him leave off this exercise. . . .

In winter he suffered very much from the frost. . . . His feet were full of sores, his legs dropsical, his knees bloody and seared, his loins covered with scars from the horsehair, his body wasted, his mouth parched with intense thirst, and his hands tremulous from weakness. Amid these torments he spent his nights and days; and he endured them all out of the greatness of the love which he bore in his heart to our Lord Jesus Christ, whose agonizing sufferings he sought to imitate.

He continued his torments for about sixteen years. At the end of this time, when his blood was now chilled, and the fire of his temperament destroyed, there appeared to him in a vision on Whitsunday, a messenger from heaven, who told him that God required this of him no longer. Whereupon he discontinued it.[8]

Thereafter Suso led what was comparatively speaking a normal life, and wrote various mystical and devotional works in which he extolled the value of 'detachment'— *i.e.* complete inner withdrawal from human contacts and the world of the senses. Among his prescriptions for achieving detachment were—'Live as if there were no creature on earth but thee', and 'Keep thy senses closed to every image which may present itself. Be empty of everything which . . . brings earthly joy or delight into the heart.'[9]

It may be said that a movement should not be judged by its lunatic fringe. But (disregarding the adjective) Suso was by no means at the fringe of the Church's life. He was for some years the Prior of a monastery; his writings exerted considerable influence both during his lifetime and in the century after his death;[10] and he still has his admirers today. The Roman Catholic weekly *The Tablet*, on the occasion of his sixth centenary in January 1966, said that though Suso has been 'singularly neglected' in Britain 'in Germany as might be expected, he is held in great respect by Catholics and Evangelicals alike'.

To move on another two centuries: a sixteenth-century Spanish saint who is still greatly revered today is St John of the Cross. Self-deprivation, rather than self-torture, was his road to sainthood. In *The Ascent of Mount Carmel* he wrote:

> The radical remedy lies in the mortification of the four great natural passions, joy, hope, fear and grief. . . . Let your soul therefore turn always:
> Not to what is most easy, but to what is hardest;
> Not to what tastes best, but to what is most distasteful;
> Not to what most pleases, but to what disgusts;
> Not to matter of consolation, but to matter for desolation rather;
> Not to rest, but to labor;
> Not to desire the more, but the less;
> Not to aspire to what is highest and most precious, but to what is lowest and most contemptible;
> Not to will anything, but to will nothing;
> Not to seek the best in everything, but to seek the worst, so that you may enter for the love of Christ into a complete destitution, a perfect poverty of spirit, and an absolute renunciation of everything in this world.[11]

By the nineteenth century the intellectual climate had

been transformed by the Enlightenment, and the ascetic tradition had greatly weakened. But it was still definitely alive in the Catholic church and among the leaders of the High Anglican movement. Thus Newman in a funeral sermon described with unqualified admiration how the deceased, the Right Rev. Henry Weedall, had continued his regime of self-mortification even on his deathbed.

> When a friend visited him in the last week, he found he had scrupled at allowing his temples to be moistened with some refreshing waters, and had with difficulty been brought to give his consent; he said he feared it was too great a luxury. When the same friend offered him some liquid to allay his distressing thirst, his answer was the same. . . . These meritorious acts are written in the Book of Life, and they have followed him whither he is gone.[12]

Pusey (1800–1882), who was the Dean of Christ Church and one of the leading figures of the High Anglican movement, was another who tried to emulate the early ascetics. His attempts at self-mortification, however, were a trifle half-hearted. As he wrote to Keble:

> I am a great coward about inflicting pain on myself, partly I hope from derangement of my nervous system; hair cloth I know not how to make pain; it is only symbolical, except when worn to an extent which seemed to wear me out. I have it on again, by God's mercy. I would try to get some sharper sort. I think I should like to be bid to use the discipline [i.e. self-scourging]. I cannot even smite on my breast much, because the pressure on my lungs seemed bad. In short, you see, I am a mass of infirmities.[13]

One cannot but feel that Pusey might have found some more worthwhile preoccupation. During the earlier part of his life, young children were working a ten-hour day in the factories, but Pusey and his fellow High Anglicans showed no interest in the campaign against child labour, just as they showed no interest in the abolition of slavery. Both these reforms were brought about largely by unbelievers—almost the only Christians who showed any interest being Quakers and Nonconformists (cf. p. 142). When the High Anglicans thought of good causes they did not think of the abolition of slavery or child labour; they thought of such things as preventing a man from marrying his deceased wife's sister. Pusey felt deeply on this subject—not from any considerations of human happiness, but because he held that certain texts in Leviticus expressly forbade such unions. But no cause, Pusey felt, must be allowed to distract him from his primary task of ensuring his own salvation. In a letter to Newman he wrote:

> I fear that often ... the consciousness of being engaged in a good cause has engrossed me too entirely, and made me think of my existence too much in reference to what might be accomplished by my means here, instead of looking pre-eminently to the preparing of myself to meet my God.[14]

It would be hard to find a more explicit statement of the self-centred other-worldliness that is of the essence of gospel Christianity.

TEN

ISLAM AND THE CRUSADES

The gradual lightening of the Dark Ages was due largely to the influence of Islam. While Europe was sunk in dogmatic slumbers, a brilliant Arab-Persian civilization was growing up in the eastern world. Most English-speaking people today are surprisingly ill-informed about this great period of Arab history; if they can recognize an allusion to the Caliph Haroun al Raschid or the poet Omar Khayyam, this is probably the extent of their knowledge. But in the ninth and tenth centuries the Arab empire was twice as large as the Roman Empire had ever been; and in many parts of this empire, above all in its eastern and western capitals Baghdad and Cordova, art, literature and science flourished in an atmosphere of considerable intellectual freedom. Great advances were made in mathematics, astronomy and medicine, and an architecture of extreme beauty developed. Furthermore, the Arabs had not lost touch, as the Christians had, with the great traditions of Greece and Rome. Many classical writers, in particular Aristotle, were well known to them and were translated into Arabic, and it was through these translations that some of the great pre-Christian writers were eventually re-introduced into Europe.

The Arab empire at its greatest extended as far west as Spain, which was conquered by the Saracens* in 712, and

* The term 'Saracen'—literally 'man of the east'—was originally applied to a predatory Arab tribe the Saraceni, but was later used to denote Muslims in general.

thereafter for some centuries was a sort of oasis of light and learning in Europe. The first contacts between the Muslim and Christian worlds occurred as a result of this conquest. The ideals of chivalry and the love of poetry and music spread northwards, chiefly through the troubadours of Provence, so that southern France became the cradle of that Romanesque, High Gothic civilization that was one of the glories of the Middle Ages. But the main source of Muslim-Christian interaction was the crusades, to which we must now turn.

By the eleventh century the boundaries of the Byzantine empire had considerably contracted as the result of pressure from both the east and the west; and towards the end of the century there appeared a new enemy, the Seljuk Turks, who attacked the provinces of Asia Minor and captured the Holy City of Jerusalem. In 1095, therefore, Alexius I appealed to Pope Urban II for help.

His appeal was favourably received. The Pope himself was less interested in recapturing Jerusalem and defending Asia Minor than in the prospect of reuniting the Eastern Orthodox and the Western Churches, which had split apart in 1054 over the question of adding the words *filioque* to the Nicene Creed.* But the idea of recapturing the holy places from the infidel made a powerful appeal to the popular imagination. It appealed to religious zeal as well as to the simple love of adventure and fighting; and it offered the certainty of eternal bliss to those who died in a holy war, together with the more mundane prospect of abundant loot for survivors. So, moved by

---

* The older Greek church held that the Holy Ghost 'proceeded from the Father', while the Latin Church added the words 'and the Son' (*filioque*), and placed the Greek church out of communion because it would not follow this lead.

these various considerations, thousands of people from all over Europe flocked to join the armies of the cross. The first to set off were little more than a horde of peasants, led by a fanatical zealot known as Peter the Hermit. Only a fraction of them reached Constantinople, and those who did were quickly wiped out by the Turks. But in 1096 a more organized force, led by various knights and barons and composed of men from all the countries of Western Europe, set out by various routes to converge on Constantinople. From there—an army some 300,000 strong—they started their attack on the Holy Land. After nearly a year's siege they captured Antioch, and a large number of the crusaders remained there, while a smaller force, under Godfrey of Bouillon, went on to Jerusalem, which they captured in 1099. The blood-bath that followed has been described by an eye-witness in the *Gesta Francorum*.

> The defenders fled along the walls and through the city, and our men pursued them killing and cutting them down as far as Solomon's temple, where there was such a massacre that our men were wading ankle-deep in blood. . . . Then the crusaders rushed round the whole city, seizing gold and silver, horses and mules, and looting the houses that were full of costly things. Then, rejoicing and weeping from excess of happiness, they all came to worship and give thanks at the sepulchre of our saviour Jesus. Next morning they went cautiously up on to the temple roof and attacked the Saracens, both men and women [who had taken refuge there], cutting off their heads with drawn swords. . . .
>
> Our leaders then gave orders that all the Saracen corpses should be thrown outside the city because of the stench, for almost the whole city was full of their

dead bodies. . . . Such a slaughter of pagans had never been seen or heard of, for they were burned in pyres like pyramids, and none save God alone knows how many there were.[1]

The Second Crusade was from the Christian point of view a disaster; in 1187 the Muslims, led by their great Sultan Saladin, mounted a counter-offensive and drove the Christians from Jerusalem. This gave rise to the Third Crusade, led by the three great rulers of Europe, the German Emperor Frederich Barbarossa, Philip Augustus of France and Richard Coeur de Lion of England. The Emperor, however, was drowned and the French and English Kings quarrelled so bitterly that little was achieved, and Jerusalem remained in Turkish hands.

The Fourth Crusade was planned by Pope Innocent III in 1201, and the Crusaders assembled in Venice. There, while in winter quarters, they were persuaded by the Venetians to abandon their original plan and to join with them in attacking their fellow-Christians in the Byzantine Empire. The ignoble enterprise succeeded, and in 1204 Constantinople was captured and the Emperor deposed. A precarious Latin Empire was established there, and lasted until 1261 when the Byzantine Christians succeeded in regaining the city.

The sorry story of the Crusades was by no means over. There were four more Crusades in the thirteenth century, the last of them led by the French King Louis IX who was later canonized. They were progressively less successful, and by 1291 all remaining Christian possessions in Syria had been recaptured by the Muslims.

ELEVEN

THE INQUISITION AND THE WARS OF RELIGION

The Crusades profoundly affected the life of Western Europe. The crusaders who returned home (and many of the survivors did not, but settled permanently in the East) had had their outlook immeasurably widened. Peasants who had never before left their native village had seen the splendours of cities like Venice and Constantinople. But, most important in the present context, they had learned to their surprise that the infidel, whom they had been taught to regard as a monster of wickedness, was often a civilized and chivalrous individual, far superior to themselves in education, magnanimity and the arts of war. To quote E. M. Hulme:

> They discovered that the Saracens were not monsters of iniquity and cruelty. The eastern infidels proved very human. When they became known as prisoners, or negotiators, or traders, they were very companionable. They were always outdoing the Westerners in generosity. At times they released prisoners without ransom. When the army of Godfrey de Bouillon entered Jerusalem it inaugurated the Kingdom of God by massacring some two thousand Jews and Moslems. When Richard I captured Jaffa he put to death the three or four hundred hostages that had been confided to him. Raymond of Toulouse tore out the eyes and cut off the arms and legs of prisoners. Such things were common

doings of the crusaders. But when Saladin retook Jerusalem he protected the Christian population; and he even supplied the refugees with food and safe-conduct to the seaboard.[1]

The superstition and intolerance of the Dark Ages could not wholly survive these contacts; the first seeds of enlightenment had been sown. But this development was far from welcome to the Church. The intellectual stagnation of the previous centuries had been entirely to her liking and she saw nothing but danger in the growing tendency of the ordinary people to think for themselves. One of the first manifestations of this tendency occurred in south-eastern France among the Cathars or Albigenses. These were the spiritual descendants of the Manicheans— followers of an ancient heresy, to which St Augustine had at one time been drawn, which held that the world is the battle-ground of a good and an evil principle. The Cathars went further, and asserted that this world is the creation of Satan and that peace and happiness are to be found only in the next world, the creation of God. The doctrine aroused disapproval because of its pessimism—though it was far less pessimistic than Augustine's later doctrine that most of the human race are damned irrevocably— but the Cathars were peaceful and law-abiding, and in the eleventh and twelfth centuries they lived comparatively unmolested, though various attempts were made to convert them peacefully to a more orthodox faith. In 1209, however, Pope Innocent III, who had launched the fourth crusade, initiated a savage persecution in which heretics were massacred wholesale and the nascent Provençal civilization was almost destroyed. Even so, the heresy was not wholly extirpated; but in 1233 the

Inquisition was founded, and this body, operating un-remittingly throughout the following century, eventually succeeded in exterminating both the heresy and the heretics.

The Inquisition was known officially as the Holy Office. It continued to operate until well into the eigh-teenth century, and it was not formally abolished until a century later. Its dreadful activities are well enough known to make it unnecessary to describe them in detail, but a few points must be made.

Though most of its worst horrors were connected with Spain, the Inquisition was by no means a purely Spanish institution as is sometimes supposed. At the outset it operated mainly in France, Germany and Italy and was not extended to Spain until the fifteenth century. But the first Spanish Inquisitor-General, Torquemada, became so notorious for his atrocities that the Spanish Inquisition tended to be identified with the Inquisition in general. How many people it tortured and killed is impossible to say with certainty. The historian Llorente, who had free access to the archives of the Spanish Inquisition, says that in Spain alone more than 31,000 persons were burned, and more than 290,000 condemned to punishments less severe than death. These estimates may be exaggerated, but if they were exaggerated tenfold they would still represent an amount of human suffering that is appalling to contemplate.

In his *Treatise on Toleration* Voltaire turned his delicate, deadly irony against the Inquisition, which in his day had still not ceased to operate in France. He imagined himself in dialogue with an inquisitor.

I would next address myself to the Christians, and

would venture to say to, for instance, a Dominican friar—an inquisitor of the faith: 'Brother, you are aware that each province in Italy has its own dialect, and that people do not speak at Venice and Bergamo as they do at Florence. The academy of La Crusca has fixed the language. Its dictionary is a rule that has to be followed, and the grammar of Matei is an infallible guide. But do you think that the consul of the Academy, or Matei in his absence, could in conscience cut out the tongues of all the Venetians and the Bergamese who persisted in speaking their own dialect?'

The inquisitor replies: 'The two cases are very different. In our case it is a question of your eternal salvation. It is for your good that the heads of the Inquisition direct that you shall be seized on the information of any one person, however infamous or criminal; that you shall have no advocate to defend you; that the name of your accuser shall not be made known to you; that the inquisitor shall promise you pardon and then condemn you; and that you shall then be subjected to five kinds of torture, and afterwards either flogged or sent to the galleys or ceremoniously burned. On this Father Ivonet, Doctor Cuchalon, Zanchinus, Campegius, Royas, Felinus, Gomarus, Diaburas and Gemelinus are explicit, and this pious practice admits of no exception.'

I would take the liberty of replying: 'Brother, possibly you are right. I am convinced that you wish to do me good. But could I not be saved without all that?'

The *Treatise on Toleration* appeared in 1763. In 1766 a young man, the Chevalier de la Barre, had his tongue torn out, his ears cut off and was then hanged, for singing blasphemous songs. In 1772 the Inquisition in France was abolished.

7

The Wars of Religion

The Inquisition was not the only instrument used by Christian against Christian. From the fifteenth century onwards, Europe was the scene of recurrent religious wars.

The first of these broke out in Bohemia. John Huss, the Rector of the University of Prague, had been greatly influenced by Wycliffe, and in 1412 he delivered a series of lectures based on Wycliffe's teaching. As a result he was excommunicated, and three years later, in 1415, he was decoyed to the Council of Constance under promise of a safe-conduct. Once there, despite the safe-conduct, he was put on trial for heresy, convicted and burned. His supporters rose against the Church, and in 1420 the Pope, Martin V, issued a bill proclaiming a crusade 'for the destruction of the Wycliffites, Hussites and all other heretics in Bohemia'. This led to a series of bloody wars which continued intermittently for some ten years.

In the century after the Reformation, wars between Catholics and Protestants were almost continuous. In 1546, soon after the death of Luther, religious wars broke out in Germany and continued until 1552. They were shortly followed by the French wars of religion. In the latter half of the sixteenth century there were no fewer than eight minor civil wars in France between the French Protestants, known as Huguenots, and the Catholics. It was in the course of these wars, in 1572, that there occurred the notorious massacre of St Bartholomew's Day, in which many hundreds (most contemporary records say thousands) of Huguenots were slaughtered in the streets of Paris, and hundreds more in other parts of France. The Pope, Gregory XIII, was so overjoyed at the news that he ordered salvos to be fired from the Castel St Angelo, and a medal to be struck commemorating the 'victory'. This medal bore on one side the Holy Father's own profile, and on the other a representation of the Angel of God cleaving the Protestants. In addition, the painter Vasari was commissioned to depict scenes of the slaughter on the walls of the Sala Regia in the Vatican.

Of all the religious wars the most destructive was the Thirty Years' War, which raged from 1618 to 1648, and involved Germany, France, Italy, Spain, Sweden and Denmark. This war reduced the population of Germany by a third—a far higher proportion than was destroyed in any of the global wars of the twentieth century.

It would be optimistic to assume that religious wars are entirely a thing of the past. Between 1941 and 1944, when Britain was too preoccupied with the war with Germany to take much note of what was going on in Yugoslavia, the Catholic Fascist movement in Croatia, known as the Ustasa, was responsible for the forcible conversion of thousands of Orthodox Serbs to Catholicism and the killing of thousands more. And at the time of writing a religious war is being waged with a typical ruthless vindictiveness in Northern Ireland. 'What does it matter if Protestants get killed? They're all bigots, aren't they?'— this comment by Sean MacStiofain,[2] the Provisional Chief of Staff of the IRA, is in the authentic tradition of the European wars of religion.

TWELVE

WITCH HUNTING

The persecution of heretics in western Christendom was accompanied by the no less savage persecution of persons accused of witchcraft. In the Dark Ages systematic witch-hunting had been unknown. The newly-converted barbarians still retained some of their old superstitions, and occasionally a suspected sorcerer was hounded to death; but Charlemagne had denounced such killing as 'a pagan practice', and made it subject to the death penalty. 'Official' witch-hunting in Europe did not begin until the fifteenth century, and was closely connected with the outbreak of heresy-hunting that followed the Crusades.

When the Albigensian heresy had been finally extirpated, the newly-established Inquisition turned its attention to witches, and in the following century there was a good deal of sporadic persecution centred mainly in southern France. But the first official mandate for witch-hunting was given in 1484, when Pope Innocent VIII issued a Bull against witchcraft and authorized two inquisitors to punish it. Two years later those same inquisitors published the first great encyclopaedia of demonology, the *Malleus Maleficarum*, 'the hammer of witches', in which witches were said to have sexual intercourse with the devil, and were accused of every other crime which a sadistic and prurient imagination could devise. Thereafter witch-hunting spread to most countries of Europe, and for more than two centuries persisted like a foul infection in the bloodstream of western Christendom—becoming latent at times but then, when circumstances favoured it, breaking out again with renewed virulence.

The Inquisition was the first and principal persecutor. But after the Reformation the Protestant Church persecuted no less zealously (Luther strongly advocated the duty of witch-burning), and from the first the ecclesiastical arm was at times reinforced by the civil authorities and by individual princes and nobles.

The cruelty of the persecution stuns the imagination. No-one accused of witchcraft had much hope of escaping alive. Usually suspects were tortured until they confessed —and the tortures employed were so dreadful that the victims were usually ready to confess to anything—and having confessed, they were then tortured again to make them incriminate others. Then they were burned. If they held out and refused to confess, they were usually burned none the less, as a penalty for obduracy. The witch craze in Europe was at its height from the middle of the fifteenth to the end of the seventeenth century. In England it was much less severe than in most other countries, and it is for this reason, probably, that few English people today realize the full horror of what occurred. The country most affected was Germany, and it is estimated that in that country alone, between 1450 and 1550, some hundred thousand alleged witches were put to death. The intensity of the persecution varied from one area to another according to the zeal of individual princes or bishops. In some districts in the Rhineland not a woman over forty was left alive; and it was said to be the prayer of young women that they would not live to old age, since if they did they were almost certain to be accused of witchcraft and die at the stake. An admiring chronicler wrote of Heinrich Julius, Duke of Brunswick, that such was his zeal for extirpating witches that the square in Wolfen-büttel looked like a little forest, so crowded were the stakes. In other areas, where the supply of firewood proved inadequate for individual burnings, large ovens were constructed in which numbers of witches could be simultaneously roasted to death.

The majority of the victims were women, but many men, and even some children, went to the stake. If a child was said to have accompanied its mother to the witches' Sabbat, the original practice was for it to be flogged in front of the fire on which its mother was burning; but it was later decided that this was too lenient, and the children were burned as well.

Among the men who suffered was Johannes Junius, burgomaster of Bamberg, and a letter has survived which he contrived to smuggle out of prison to his daughter:

Many hundred thousand good-nights, dearly beloved daughter Veronica. Innocent have I come to prison, innocent have I been tortured, innocent must I die. For whoever comes into the witch prison must become a witch or be tortured until he invents something out of his head and—God pity him, bethinks him of something. I will tell you how it has gone with me . . . the executioner . . . put the thumbscrews on me, that the blood ran out at the nails and everywhere, so that for four weeks I could not use my hands as you can see from the writing. . . . Thereafter they first stripped me, bound my hands behind me, and drew me up in the torture. Then I thought Heaven and Earth were at an end; eight times did they draw me up and let me fall again, so that I suffered terrible agony. The executioner said: 'Sir, I beg you for God's sake confess something, whether it be true or not, for you cannot endure the torture which you will be put to, and even if you bear it all, yet you will not escape.'

Burgomaster Junius asked for a day to think again, invented a story of a witch meeting and, under threat of further torture, named various people as being present; he also admitted to other crimes. The letter goes on:

> Now, dear child, here you have all my confession, for which I must die. And they are sheer lies and made-up things, so help me God. For all this I was forced to say through fear of the torture which was threatened beyond what I had already endured. For they never leave off with the torture till one confesses something; be he ever so good, he must be a witch. Nobody escapes. . . .

On the margin of his letter the burgomaster had also written:

> Dear child, six have confessed against me at once: the Chancellor, his son . . . all false, through compulsion, as they have told me, and begged my forgiveness in God's name before they were executed.[1]

These horrors did not pass entirely without protest. But those who protested did not question the reality of witchcraft—to do so, indeed, would have been to court death for heresy. They merely argued that confessions obtained under torture were worthless, and that many of those convicted of witchcraft were in fact innocent. Thus a Jesuit, Friedrich Spee, whose hair had been turned prematurely white by his experience as a confessor of witches in the great persecution at Würzburg, wrote in 1631 'Torture fills our Germany with witches and unheard-of wickedness. . . . If all of us have not confessed ourselves witches, that is only because we have not all been tortured.'[2]

Even such protests as this required considerable courage, and though Spee himself escaped, many who protested were themselves accused of witchcraft and burned. And it must be sadly recorded that their protests had little effect. As Voltaire memorably said, men who believe absurdities will commit atrocities; and so long as men believed in a devil who operated through human agents, witch-hunting was bound to continue and humane protests could at most slightly mitigate its savagery.

Disbelief in witchcraft was from the first regarded as heretical. Thus the *Malleus Maleficarum*, the earliest treatise on demonology, bore on its title page the epigraph *Haeresis est maxima opera maleficarum non credere*— 'to disbelieve in witchcraft is the greatest of heresies'— and it continued to be so regarded until the seventeenth century, when scepticism for the first time began to be openly expressed, at all events in England. Such scepticism was rightly regarded by the orthodox as the thin end of the wedge, and was met with the strongest disapproval. Thus Joseph Glanvil, a distinguished Protestant divine, wrote in 1666 in *Sadducismus Triumphatus*: 'Those who dare not bluntly say there is no God, content themselves . . . to deny there are spirits or witches, which sort of infidels, though they are not ordinary among the mere vulgar, yet are they numerous in a little higher rank of understandings. . . . Most of the looser gentry and the small pretenders to philosophy and wit, are generally deriders of the belief of witches and apparitions.' Sir Thomas Browne in his famous book *Religio Medici* (1643) said that those who denied witches were by implication denying spirits, and were therefore 'obliquely and upon consequence a sort, not of infidels, but of atheists'. And Ralph Cudworth, a leading philosopher and divine and a Cambridge Professor, wrote in his *True Intellectual System of the Universe* (1678): 'As for wizards and magicians . . . besides the Scriptures there hath been so full an attestation given to them . . . in all ages, that those our so confident exploders of them in this present age can hardly escape the suspicion of having some hankering towards atheism.' And it is in fact true, as Lecky pointed out, that disbelief in witches was at first almost entirely confined to men who were avowed freethinkers.

In the eighteenth century, 'the age of reason', the belief was at last outgrown; the grotesque demonology that had survived so tenaciously from the Middle Ages faded in the clear air of the Enlightenment like the memory of a nightmare at sunrise. 'Faded', however, is perhaps too strong a word, since occasional witch-burnings still took place (the last in Great Britain is thought to have occurred in Scotland in 1722), and there were still a few who clung to the old superstition. Thus in 1768 John Wesley wrote in his Journal that those who disbelieved in witchcraft were 'in direct opposition, not only to the Bible, but to the suffrage of the wisest and best of men in all ages and nations. . . . The giving up of witchcraft is in effect giving up the Bible.' And even today the Anglican Church has not made up its mind about demons. In 1958 the Archbishop's Commission on the Church's Ministry of Healing expressed itself as 'divided as to whether or not demons may cause or complicate any malady';[3] and in 1972 a Commission convened by the Bishop of Exeter recommended that every diocesan bishop should appoint a priest as diocesan exorcist, and that centres of training in exorcism should be established in every province.[4]

THIRTEEN

THE PERSECUTION OF THE JEWS

Jews in Christendom were subject to almost continuous persecution from the time of Constantine until the French Revolution.

As a minority who refused to be wholly assimilated, Jews after the dispersion were inevitably regarded with some distrust, and in the early Church distrust was increased to hostility by the belief that the Jews were responsible for the death of Jesus. The Fathers of the Church vied with one another in denouncing the Jews and declaring that they had been disinherited and rejected by God. Thus St John Chrysostom ('golden-mouthed', a name bestowed on him on account of his 'golden' eloquence) said of the synagogue: 'Let anyone call it brothel, home of vice, refuge of the devil, citadel of Satan, corruption of souls, abyss of corruption and all mischief—whatever he may say, it will be less than it has deserved.'[1]

After the conversion of Rome, the hostility of the Church began to express itself in legal enactments. Constantine began comparatively mildly, by imposing penalties for mixed marriages and conversions to Judaism. Theodosius II forbade Jews to hold any public office or to build new synagogues; and the great Civil Code of the Emperor Justinian embodied further anti-Jewish legislation, which later found its way into the law books of most European states.

In the Middle Ages, discrimination and oppression intensified. Jews had to wear a distinctive dress, and were forced to live in a separate quarter of the town, later known as the ghetto. They were excluded from almost all occupations except pawnbroking and moneylending, and denounced for usury when they practised these occupations successfully. Incredible charges were made against them, as that they engaged in the ritual murder of Christian boys at Passovertide. Mass murders of Jews became increasingly frequent. At the time of the abortive Crusade of Peter the Hermit, one of the bands of peasants en route for Constantinople demonstrated their zeal against the infidel by massacring hundreds of Jews in the Rhineland. But the worst of the persecutions occurred at the time of the Black Death, the great plague that ravaged Europe between 1347 and 1349. The Jews (whose better sanitary habits made them less liable to infection than their neighbours) were the inevitable scapegoats; they were accused of causing the plague by poisoning the wells, and a series of bloody pogroms ensued, in which thousands perished.

Jews were expelled from England in 1290 and were not readmitted until the time of Cromwell. In 1306 they were similarly expelled from France. Increasingly, therefore, they tended to withdraw to the east, particularly to Turkey and Poland. In the west their principal haven had long been Spain, where the Muslims, who had no historical grounds for intolerance, welcomed their contribution to the life of the community. To quote Cecil Roth 'Their linguistic and financial abilities won them high place in the administration. [In the tenth century] there was a remarkable renascence, in which the old traditions of the schools of Palestine and Mesopotamia, the manifold interests of the Moors, and the rediscovered sciences of ancient Greece were remarkably blended.'[2]

But, unhappily for the Jews, from the eleventh century Spain began to be re-Christianized as one Muslim area after another was reconquered by Christian armies. For a time the Christians were reasonably tolerant, but with the growth of the crusading spirit the familiar tale of oppression and persecution began again. By 1290 only Granada remained to the Moors, and in 1492 that too fell, and the last refuge of the Jews was destroyed.

Torquemada, the Spanish Inquisitor-General, was then at the height of his career. He was determined that Jews should be completely expelled from Spain, but he had not the power to expel them himself, since the Inquisition was formed to deal with heresy, and the Jews, as unbelievers, were not subject to its authority; heresy is a crime of Christians. But Torquemada employed all his powers of persuasion to induce the Queen, Isabella, to pronounce the edict of banishment. Tradition has it that the Jews offered a 'ransom' of 30,000 ducats to be allowed to remain, and that the Queen was at first disposed to accept it; but Torquemada confronted her at the door of the palace with a crucifix in his hand, exclaiming 'Judas sold his God for thirty pieces of silver—you are about to sell him for thirty thousand!' Whether or not this story is true, the edict was passed; Jews were ordered to leave Spain within three months or to accept Christian baptism. The number who chose exile has been estimated at over 150,000. Of these, thousands fell into the hands of the pirates who swarmed around the coasts, and were plundered and reduced to slavery; thousands more died of starvation, disease or drowning. Of those who survived, most made their way, after incredible hardships, to the

Muslim countries of the eastern Mediterranean, particularly Turkey.

The Jews who accepted baptism (known as Marranos) had gained a short respite, but their position was still terribly precarious; for, having become nominally Christian, they were now subject to the Inquisition, and were liable at any time to be condemned for heresy on the ground that they still secretly adhered to the Jewish faith. For a time they continued a surreptitious existence, paying lip-service to Christianity but handing on their Jewish traditions in secret from generation to generation at the risk of their lives. But by the seventeenth century persecution had become so intense that many fled to the East, or to European countries such as England or Holland where greater tolerance prevailed.

For a time the Renaissance brought some improvement in the lot of the Jews. But it was short-lived; at the Reformation things became worse than before. The Catholic Church, true to tradition, blamed the Jews for the Reformation, and the process of liberalization that had shown signs of beginning went rapidly into reverse. Hitherto the Popes had in general been less fanatical than the priests, and by the Renaissance the Jews in Italy were accorded, in Cecil Roth's phrase, a sort of contemptuous tolerance. But the threat posed by the Reformation changed all this. The oppressive medieval legislation which had been gradually falling into desuetude was revived. Jews were expelled from most of the Papal states, and, where they were allowed to remain, confined strictly to the ghettos. A number of burnings took place, and throughout Italy all discoverable copies of the Talmud were publicly destroyed.

Under the Protestants the Jews fared no better. Luther

had begun with high hopes that the purified faith of the Reformation would prove acceptable to the Jews and that they would be converted to Christianity. When this hope proved groundless his attitude changed to bitter hostility. In the words of his most recent biographer, Canon James Atkinson, Luther 'made some unpleasant remarks about the Jews. . . . [His] attack was primarily theological rather than anti-Semitic, but he was not beyond criticism at this point.'[3] In the light of Luther's treatise *On the Jews and their Lies* this seems a considerable understatement. Luther wrote:

> Beware then of the Jews, and know that a Jewish school is nothing other than a nest of the devil. . . . And when you see or hear a Jew teaching, then realize that you are hearing a venomous basilisk that can poison or kill people with the sight of his face.[4]

His more specific recommendations about the appropriate treatment of Jews included the following:

> First, that their schools and synagogues shall be set on fire. . . . Second, that their houses too shall be destroyed. . . . Third, that they shall be deprived of their prayer-books and Talmuds, which teach such idolatry, lies, cursing and blasphemy. . . . Fourth, that their rabbis shall be forbidden to teach, on pain of death. . . . Fifth, that Jews shall be deprived of safe-conduct and permission to use the roads. For, being neither landowners nor officials nor merchants nor the like, they have no business in the countryside and should remain in the ghetto. . . . Sixth, that they shall be forbidden to practise usury and shall be deprived of all their cash and their jewellery of silver and gold. . . .

And seventh, that all strong young Jews and Jewesses shall be given flails, axes and spades and made to earn their living by the sweat of their brow.[4]

And again:

It is intolerable to us Christians that a Jew's filthy mouth should utter the name of God in our presence. And if anyone should hear a Jew speak that name, let him inform the authorities, or throw pig-shit at him and drive him away. And let no-one show any mercy or kind-heartedness in this matter.[4]

It was clearly not without good reason that Julius Streicher, editor of *Der Stürmer*, cited Luther's example in his defence before the tribunal at Nüremberg.

The liberation of Jewry began with the Enlightenment and the French Revolution. After the Revolution the principle of *liberté*, *egalité*, *fraternité* was soon taken to its logical conclusion, and in 1791 a motion for the enfranch-izement of the Jews in France was carried almost without opposition in the National Assembly. The spirit of emancipation was later spread to other countries by the armies of Napoleon; and thereafter, despite periods of reaction, the trend throughout Europe was towards reducing discrimination and increasingly incorporating the Jews in the life of the community. The process took a long time (it was not until 1858, for example, that Jews were allowed to sit in the British parliament[*]). But by

* Pusey described this measure as 'anti-Christian' and as 'putting great difficulties in the way of those who are required to pray for Parliament'. As he said in a letter to Gladstone, 'I could pray for it only as apostate, and as having prepared by this step for the coming of Antichrist' (Liddon, *Life*, vol. III., p. 175).

the early years of this century it might seem to have been completed—until the Nazi revolution set the clock back three hundred years.

Under the Nazis the Jews for the first time were being persecuted by the civil authorities and not by the Church, and the Church, if it had protested, might have done something to redeem its deplorable record. But it did little or nothing. A few maverick individual Christians, such as Dietrich Bonhoeffer, became under-cover resistance workers and lost their lives. But the Pope, though he gave asylum to exiled Jews in Italy, made no official statement denouncing the persecutions, and the German Churches came near to condoning them. On the attitude of the Catholic Church I quote Archbishop T. D. Roberts, S.J.

> The overwhelming impression left on me by a careful study of Dr Gordon Zahn's *German Catholics & Hitler's Wars* is not so much shock at finding Hitler echoed over the signatures of great Catholic names: it is much more the realization that nationalism, mass hysteria, and above all, fear, paralyze Christian judgement. . . . The factual evidence seems overwhelming that German Catholics generally—bishops, clergy, people—supported the Hitler war effort.[5]

On the attitude of the Protestant Church the following passage speaks for itself: it is an extract from a declaration made in 1941 by leaders of the German Evangelical Church.

> The National Socialist leaders of Germany have provided indisputable documentary evidence that the Jews are responsible for this war in its world-wide magnitude. They have therefore . . . taken the necessary

8

steps . . . to ensure that the life of the German nation is protected against Judaism.

As members of that same German nation, the under-signed leaders of the German Evangelical Church stand in the forefront of this historical struggle to defend our country, because of which it has been necessary for the national police to issue a statement to the effect that the Jews are the enemies of the German nation and of the world, just as it was also necessary for Dr Martin Luther to demand, on the basis of his own bitter experience, that the severest measures should be taken against the Jews and that they should be expelled from all German countries.

. . . Christian baptism does not change in any way the Jew's racial character. . . . It is the duty of a German Evangelical Church to foster and to promote the religious life of the German people. Christians who are Jews by race have no place in that Church and no right to a place.[6]

Jews may be pardoned a certain bitterness when they hear Christians proclaim—as they not infrequently do—that the Nazi persecution of the Jews provides an appalling example of what happens when a nation abandons Christian standards.

FOURTEEN

THE CONDONATION OF CRUELTY

Heretics, witches, Jews—these head the list in the dreadful catalogue of the main victims of Christian superstition and intolerance. And those who ask how such atrocious cruelties could have been perpetrated in the name of the religion of love have not far to look for the answer. The religion of love was also the religion of hell-fire; and a sincere belief that sinners are tortured for ever must inevitably blunt the sensibilities and corrupt the morals of those who hold it.

The doctrine of hell provides a rational defence for even the worst cruelties of the Inquisition. For if a few hours or days of torture can induce a heretic to recant, and thus save him from everlasting torture in the life to come, then clearly the torturer has done him a service. And if the victim is obdurate and dies in his error, the agonies he endured before death are merely a brief foretaste of, and a negligible addition to, the torments he will endure thereafter for all eternity.

The doctrine could also be held to justify one of the most evil features of life in the ages of faith—the sadistic pleasure taken by people in general in the spectacle of torture. It could be argued that since our Heavenly Father has decreed that the wicked shall suffer eternally, their suffering is clearly a good thing; so it is right and proper for the virtuous to enjoy the spectacle it provides. Did not St Thomas Aquinas, the 'angelic doctor' (cf. p. 51) say that the happiness of the blest in heaven would be enhanced by their unrestricted view of the agonies of the damned in hell?

It can hardly be a coincidence that the decline of the belief in hell has been accompanied by a profound change in the general attitude to cruelty, which is now widely regarded as one of the worst of sins. This may seem a paradoxical statement, in view of the current tendency to depict cruelty and violence on film and TV. But the sadistic episodes that sicken most members of the audience, and give rise to indignant protests, when they are mimicked on the screen, were enacted daily in grim earnest in the ages of faith—and watched by gloating crowds as a form of amusement.

One of the most popular of these spectacles was the *auto-da-fé*—literally 'act of faith', a cynically euphemistic term for mass burnings at the stake. In Spain such holocausts sometimes provided a special attraction at the celebrations following a royal marriage, or the birth of an heir to the throne. In 1680 Madrid was the scene of a spectacular *auto-da-fé* arranged in honour of the wedding of the young King Charles II to the French Princess Marie Louise of Orleans. Eighty-six Jews were burned in the presence of the king, his bride, and the court and clergy of Madrid. Lecky describes a remarkable painting which in his day hung in the gallery of Madrid, depicting the procession of the Jews to the stake.

The great square was arranged like a theatre, and thronged with ladies in court dress; the king sat on an elevated platform surrounded by the chief members of the aristocracy, and Bishop Valdares, the Inquisitor-General, presided over the scene. The painter, Francesco Rizzi, has directed the sympathies of the spectators against the Jews by the usual plan of exaggerating the Jewish nose.[1]

The Marquise de Villars, who as a lady-in-waiting to the bride was a reluctant spectator of the holocaust, wrote to her husband in France:

It was a horrifying scene. The cruelties committed in the course of the execution of these unfortunates mock description. Only a medical certificate or severe illness excused attendance at the *auto-da-fé*; lacking that, to be absent incurred the risk of falling into the odour of heresy. Some even took offence that I failed to express enthusiasm for what was taking place.[2]

A Catholic radio critic, Mary Crozier, wrote in 1958: 'The atrocities of Nazi and Communist prison camps have shown up phrases like "the cruelty of the Middle Ages" as thoughtless or ignorant nonsense.'[3] This complacent judgment could not survive an impartial reading of history. No-one would wish to minimize the horrors of the prison camps, but as compared to the activities of the Inquisition the extermination policies of the Nazis seem almost humane. The Jews in the gas chambers at least died quickly and relatively painlessly. They were not burned until after their death; the Inquisition burned its victims alive. Moreover, the Nazis had to conceal what they were doing for fear of popular indignation—it is said that most ordinary Germans knew little or nothing of what went on behind the walls of the concentration camps. But in the ages of faith, watching the dying agonies of witches, Jews and heretics was a popular form of public entertainment, provided and encouraged by the Church.

FIFTEEN

GLADIATORIAL SHOWS

The previous chapters have dealt with some of the nastier aspects of Christianity's historical record. Christians, when their attention is drawn to these, say usually that they were the fruit, not of true Christianity, but of the errors and sins of its human exponents; and that in any case their evil is outweighed by the good done by the Christian religion in other fields. It is time, therefore, to consider whether this claim can be justified.

The principal achievements claimed for historical Christianity are that it kept learning alive in the monasteries during the Dark Ages and fostered education in the centuries that followed; abolished gladiatorial shows; improved the position of women; and brought about the abolition of slavery. The first of these claims will be most conveniently discussed in the final chapter of this book, but the remaining three will be examined now.

A gladiatorial show is obviously a far less cruel and corrupting spectacle than an *auto-da-fé*, so it is paradoxical that the Church which denounced the one should have approved the other. But the earliest Christians were far less bloodthirsty than their successors. They took the commandment 'thou shalt not kill' with the utmost seriousness, and until around the end of the second century they carried it to its logical conclusion by refusing to serve in the army. Thus when they condemned gladiatorial shows they did so primarily on the ground that they involved the sin of murder. To the pagans this aspect was less important; and they excused the cruelty of the games (in so far as they felt that excuse was needed) on the ground that they provided the spectators with an inspiring example of courage and indifference to death. Thus Cicero wrote:

> A gladiatorial show is apt to seem cruel and inhuman to some eyes, and I incline to think that it is so, as now conducted. But in the days when it was criminals who crossed swords in the death struggle,★ there could be no better schooling against pain and death. . . . What gladiator of ordinary merit has ever uttered a groan or changed countenance? . . . Who after falling has drawn in his neck when ordered to suffer the fatal stroke?† Such is the force of training, practice and habit.[1]

This was written in the last years of the Republic, before the passion for gladiatorial shows had taken so strong a hold on the Roman mob. By the second century it would have been quite unrealistic to defend these combats on the ground that they provided object-lessons in courage and fortitude. They had become brutal and demoralizing spectacles, and the best of the pagans avoided them or, like the Emperor Marcus Aurelius,

★ As this statement implies, when the games first began most gladiators were condemned criminals; but at a later period prisoners of war were conscripted to the arena, and there grew up also a class of professional gladiators who had embraced the profession voluntarily.

† In his own death Cicero was true to his principles. He was proscribed by Antony after the murder of Caesar, and was fleeing from Rome in a litter when he was overtaken. He thrust his neck as far forward as he could out of the litter and bade the executioners do their work.

attended reluctantly as a matter of duty and tried not to watch. But there were still remarkably few overt protests from the pagan side. The strongest came from the Stoic, Seneca, and even he concentrated his indignation mainly on the practice of forcing condemned criminals to fight without shield or armour. He described how he visited the amphitheatre during the luncheon interval, expecting the kind of light entertainment that was usually put on at that time to save the spectators from boredom. Instead he found that they were being regaled with butchery.

I expected some humour and relaxation, something in which men's eyes could find rest after a glut of human blood. But it was quite otherwise. In the previous bouts some mercy had been shown, but now all the trifling is put aside and it is butchery pure and simple. The men have nothing to protect them; their bodies are exposed at every point, and every thrust finds its mark. Many people prefer this sort of thing to the normal contest. . . . What is the point [they feel] of defensive armour, or of skill in swordsmanship? These only delay death. . . . But, [the spectator argues] this fellow was a highway robber; he killed a man. Well then, as a murderer he deserved his punishment; but what crime have you, wretched man, committed that you should have to watch it? Can you not understand even this, that bad examples recoil on those who set them?[2]

Similar language was used in the fourth century by Lactantius, who has been called the Christian Cicero. He wrote: 'For he who reckons it a pleasure that a man, though justly condemned, should be slain in his sight, pollutes his conscience as much as if he should become a spectator and a sharer of a homicide which is secretly committed. And yet they call these sports in which human blood is shed. So far has the feeling of humanity departed.'[3]

But the Fathers of the Church were not all as high-minded as Lactantius. Their protests were sometimes made, not primarily on humanitarian grounds but as part and parcel of their objection to public spectacles and entertainments of all kinds. The 'games', so-called, did not, of course, consist only of gladiatorial combats; they included chariot-racing, athletic contests, plays and other entertainments, and to the more puritanical of the Fathers these were all equally wicked. They (the Fathers) felt that Christians were best employed sitting quietly at home reflecting on their sins and the after-life; not putting on their best clothes and going out to enjoy themselves with their friends. Thus Tertullian (150–230) (described in the *Oxford Dictionary of the Christian Church* as 'standing beside St Augustine as the greatest Western theologian of the patristic period') wrote:

Nothing connected with the games pleases God. . . . The spectacles one and all were instituted for the devil's sake, and equipped from the devil's stores. . . . Do you think that, seated where there is nothing of God [a man] will at that moment turn his thoughts to God? Peace of soul will be his, I take it, as he shouts for the charioteer? With his mind on the actors, he will learn purity? No, in all the show there will be nothing more sure to trip him up than the mere over-nice attire of women and men. That sharing of emotions, that agreement or disagreement in backing their favourites, makes an intercourse that fans the sparks of lust. . . . You are too dainty, O Christian, if you long for pleasure in this world as well as the other.[4]

Tertullian concluded his diatribe with some zestful anticipations of the Last Judgment:

> What sight shall wake my wonder, what my laughter, my joy and exultation? . . . The poets trembling before the judgment seat, not of Rhadamanthus, not of Minos, but of Christ. . . . And then there will be the tragic actors to be heard, more vocal in their own tragedy; and the players to be seen, lither of limb by far in the fire; and then the charioteers to watch, red all over in the wheel of flame; and next the athletes to be gazed upon, not in their gymnasiums, but hurled in the fire. . . . Such sights, such exultation![4]

It would be surprising if the author of this 'infernal description', in Gibbon's phrase, were much disturbed by the cruelties of the arena.

It was not until nearly ninety years after the conversion of Rome that the shows were finally abolished. But it can be said with some confidence that they would have lasted still longer under paganism. As Lecky put it, 'Christianity alone was powerful enough to tear this evil plant from the Roman soil.'[5] But the evil plant proved at first extremely tenacious. In 325, five years before the capital was transferred to Constantinople, Constantine issued the first official edict condemning the games. But it had little effect except in Constantinople itself, where gladiatorial shows never took root, being replaced by a passion for horse-racing. Elsewhere in the East, and throughout the Western Empire, things at first went on much as before. The Church, however, kept up its steady pressure, refusing to admit any professional gladiator to baptism unless he renounced his calling, and excluding from communion all Christians who attended the games, until gradually the climate of opinion changed. The last gladiatorial show was held in Rome under the Emperor Honorius, at a date variously stated as 391 and 404. The story runs that Honorius was moved to abolish the games by the action of a monk, Telemachus, who ran into the arena and tried to part the combatants, and was stoned to death by the angry spectators. But this story is probably fictitious. If an event so dramatic and with such far-reaching consequences had really occurred, one would expect it to be widely described and acclaimed in Christian writings. But in fact the only references to it are a few lines in Theodoret's *Ecclesiastical History* (V, 26), and a note in the *Hieronymian Martyrology* (a sort of register of Christian martyrs), in which the monk is called Almachius.

A particularly unconvincing feature of the story is the statement that the monk was killed by stoning. Where, one wonders, did the spectators get the stones? Had they brought them in with them, or did they find them lying around among the seats in the amphitheatre? Neither explanation seems probable.

But even though Telemachus must be classed with William Tell, and even though gladiatorial shows were not finally abolished until nearly a century after the conversion of Rome, there is justice in the claim that their abolition was due primarily to Christianity. Equal justice does not attach to the next two claims to be considered.

SIXTEEN

THE POSITION OF WOMEN

It is impossible to generalize about the position of women in the many great civilizations that existed before Christianity. In the earliest cultures of which we have much knowledge—those of Babylonia and of ancient Egypt, which flourished in and around the twentieth century BC—women appear to have held an honourable position and to have played a full part in both public and family life: in Egypt many of the rulers were women. And ten centuries later, in the Homeric age in Greece, women, as depicted in the *Iliad* and the *Odyssey*, led lives that were both free and dignified.

By contrast, in the fifth century BC in the Athens of Pericles (though not in Sparta) women were an un-privileged class. They received less education than men, they could not vote in the Assembly, and they were subordinated to their husbands in marriage. Aristotle in the *Politics* explained that by nature the male is superior and the female inferior, hence the male rules and the woman is ruled.

Less is known about the position of women in the first great age of Chinese civilization, under the Han dynasty which lasted from about 200 BC to 200 AD. But the fact that several Empresses reigned during this period suggests that women's status was considerably higher than in Athens.

In considering the Christian claim to have improved

the position of women I shall not attempt to amplify, or qualify, the above outline, oversimplified though it is. I will concentrate instead on what is beyond doubt the most relevant comparison—namely that between the position of women in pagan Rome before the conversion of Constantine, and their position after Rome had become Christian.

On this subject I will quote two authorities. First, L. J. Hobhouse, in his lifetime Professor of Sociology in the University of London:

> The Roman matron of the Empire was more fully her own mistress than the married woman of any earlier civilization with the possible exception of a certain period of Egyptian history, and it must be added, than the wife of any later civilization down to our own generation.[1]

Second, Sir James Donaldson, who in his lifetime was Professor of Latin at the University of Aberdeen and later Principal of the University of St Andrews. He wrote:

> At the time when Christianity dawned on the world women had attained ... great freedom, power and influence in the Roman Empire. ... Women had been liberated from the enslaving fetters of the old legal forms, and they enjoyed freedom of intercourse in society; ... they dined in the company of men, they studied literature and philosophy, they took part in political movements, they were allowed to defend their own law cases if they liked, and they helped their husbands in the governing of provinces and the writing of books.[2]

In the later years of the Empire, the system of marriage was such as would, one imagines, receive the whole-hearted approval of Women's Lib today. Marriage depended on a simple mutual agreement, unaccompanied by any civil or religious ceremony. The wife did not pass under the rule of her husband; in the eyes of the law she remained a member of her father's family and under her father's guardianship, but the old *patria potestas* had long since become a dead letter, and in effect the wife was completely independent. Apart from her dowry, which passed into the hands of her husband (but which was returned to the wife if the marriage ended in divorce) she held her property in her own right; and this property might well be considerable, since in matters of inheritance it was rare for any distinction to be made between sons and daughters. Thus a considerable portion of Roman wealth was controlled by women, and the tyranny exercised by some rich wives over their husbands was a popular theme of satirists.

Marriage was monogamous and adultery was frowned upon. Divorce, however, was common, at all events among the propertied classes. Marriage, being contracted by mutual consent, could be dissolved by mutual consent —indeed the consent need not even be mutual, since either partner could repudiate the contract at will and this led automatically to divorce, giving both parties the right to re-marry. This certainly impaired the stability of marriage, and led to a situation of serial monogamy resembling that which obtains today in circles, such as the aristocracy and the stage, where women are usually financially independent. Whether or not this was a bad thing is a matter for argument, but there can be no doubt that women, under the pagan emperors, enjoyed a prestige and independence almost unparalleled in history. Their position deteriorated steadily as the influence of Christianity advanced.

Two influences in particular have contributed to forming the Christian attitude towards women. First, the creation story in Genesis, which implies that woman is man's natural subordinate, created to serve and obey him: and, second, the myth of the virgin birth, which has encouraged the view that sex is unclean and displeasing to God.

The Old Testament is, of course, the common heritage of Judaism and Christianity, and both these religions were at first strongly patriarchal in outlook—though Judaism, on the whole, rather less so than its offshoot. The Christian view about the proper behaviour for women in church and at home was for centuries based on the injunctions of Paul.

> Let your women keep silence in the churches: for it is not permitted unto them to speak; but they are commanded to be under obedience, as also saith the law. And if they will learn any thing, let them ask their husbands at home: for it is a shame for women to speak in the church.
>
> (I Cor. xiv, 34–5)

> Wives, submit yourselves unto your own husbands, as unto the Lord. For the husband is the head of the wife, even as Christ is the head of the church. . . . Therefore as the church is subject unto Christ, so let the wives be to their own husbands, in every thing.
>
> (Eph. v, 22–24)

Judaism never went quite to these lengths. The Jews it

is true, excluded women from public life and relegated them to a special section of the synagogue; but in the home, which has always been the centre of Jewish life, the wife was supreme—so much so that the Jewish matriarch is almost as much of a type-figure as the Roman matron. Neither type has any counterpart in Christianity.

It is in their attitude to the family that Judaism and Christianity differ most widely. Judaism has never depreciated marriage nor regarded sex as unclean. It has never had a celibate priesthood—on the contrary, the High Priest was not allowed to perform the solemn service of the Day of Atonement unless he had a wife 'to make his home holy'. The warmth and security of home and family have been an abiding feature of Jewish life throughout the centuries, and doubtless did much to help the persecuted Jews to withstand the near-intolerable conditions to which they were subjected outside it. The attitude of the early Christians was very different, as has already been indicated in Chapter 9; and one of the main factors responsible for the difference has been the specifically Christian doctrine of the virgin birth, which has done more than is generally realized to influence the Christian attitude towards women.

There is no trace of this story in the earliest Christian documents. It is not referred to in the gospel of Mark, dating from about 70 AD, and Paul clearly knew nothing of it. The development of the legend runs concurrently with the growth of the tendency to regard Jesus, not simply as the Jewish Messiah, but as the incarnation of God. If Jesus was indeed a divine Being, it was impossible to regard him simply as the son of two Jewish peasants. A supernatural Being must have had a supernatural origin; and since the gospel stories clearly indicate that

Jesus was conceived outside wedlock (it has been suggested, not unplausibly, that his father was a Roman soldier), a divine parentage and a virgin birth was a natural form for the developing legend to take. It is not suggested, of course, that the story was a conscious invention. In a superstitious and credulous age legends do not need to be invented; they arise by a process more akin to organic growth. The story, moreover, was entirely in accordance with current tradition. In Greek and Roman mythology, gods and goddesses were frequently said to have been begotten or born in unusual ways. Aphrodite rose from the sea; Mithras, the sun-god, was born from the cleft of a rock; Athena sprang from the head, and Dionysus from the thigh, of Zeus; and Hera, the wife and sister of Zeus, gave birth to Hephaestus without his co-operation. Similar claims were often made for demigods—i.e. the offspring of a god and a mortal, a category to which the Jesus of legend, strictly speaking, belongs. Thus the deified emperor Augustus was said to have been miraculously begotten upon his mother by a snake in the temple of Apollo; Perseus was born to the (presumably) still virginal Danae after Zeus had descended upon her in the form of a shower of gold; and the twin gods Castor and Pollux, begotten upon Leda by Zeus in the form of a swan, were said to have been hatched from eggs.

The story of the conception and birth of Jesus, though less bizarre, belongs clearly to the same tradition. The first reference to it in Christian writings is in the gospel of Matthew, dating from around 90 AD. But here either the text is corrupt or the writer was in considerable confusion, since the Gospel begins by tracing Jesus' ancestry back through his father, Joseph, in order to demonstrate that he was of the house of David, then goes on immedia-

9

tely to state that Jesus was not the son of Joseph, but was conceived by the Holy Ghost.

It is in the gospel of Luke, roughly contemporary with Matthew, that the story reaches its full development. In Luke, and in Luke alone, we get the romantic and moving stories of the annunciation and the nativity that have so seized on the imagination of the world. Innocent and beautiful legendary accretions, it might be thought, in harmony with the spirit of the age. But the implication that none but a virgin was worthy to be the mother of Jesus has had a deplorable effect on the Church's attitude to women; for it inevitably reinforced the belief, already foreshadowed in the sayings of Jesus and Paul, that marriage and sex are impure.

The view of the Early Fathers—not shared by the Jews —appears to have been that our sex and reproductive arrangements were the result of, if not actually a punishment for, the disobedience of Adam and Eve; thus St Jerome wrote 'Eve in Paradise was a virgin. . . . Understand that virginity is natural and that marriage came after the Fall.'[3] Some of the sayings of Jesus and of Paul could be held to support this view (cf. pp. 43–4). But neither Jesus nor Paul approached the pathological sex-hatred displayed by some of the saints and theologians of the patristic era, to whom woman was the cause of the Fall, the source of temptation, the agent by which sex and its attendant evils came into the world. If a woman in the Dark Ages was to achieve any status or dignity it was essential that she should renounce sex. Nuns, vowed to celibacy, held a recognized and honourable place in the community, and if an able woman entered a convent she could attain a position of authority as an abbess or prioress. But woman as an actual or potential sex partner was, in the words of St John Chrysostom (4th–5th century) 'a necessary evil, a natural temptation, a desirable calamity, a domestic peril, a deadly fascination and a painted ill'.[4]

Women not dedicated to virginity were regarded as so unclean that it was only with strict precautions that they could be allowed to participate in the rites of the Church. They were not, needless to say, permitted to sing in cathedral choirs;* and when part-singing emerged in the Middle Ages, the necessary higher tones were provided by boys and by male *castrati*, whose mutilation was evidently considered a lesser evil than the admission of female singers. Women were enjoined not to come near the altar while mass was celebrating, and an edict of the sixth century forbade them to receive the eucharist into their bare hands.

But it was in their pronouncements about sex and marriage that the Fathers of the Church went to their greatest extremes. Thus Tertullian (150–230), that esteemed theologian whose views on the games have already been quoted, drew no distinction between marriage and fornication. He wrote: 'Marriage and fornication are different only because laws appear to make them so. . . . In the shameful act which constitutes its essence, marriage is the same as fornication. Therefore "it is best for a man not to touch a woman".'[5]

Later theologians did not go quite so far. St Jerome (340–420) realized that even virgins must have mothers, and wrote 'I praise wedlock, I praise marriage, but it is

---

* This prohibition lasted for centuries. As late as 1872 Dr Manning, then Cardinal Archbishop of Westminster, issued a circular to the clergy of his diocese ordering them to discontinue the employment of female vocalists in their church choirs.

because they produce me virgins.'[6] But it was St Augustine (354–430)—that prince of the Church who in his youth prayed 'Oh Lord, make me chaste, but not yet'—who expounded most fully the doctrine that has done so much to poison the wellsprings of human happiness. Augustine explained that the lusts of the flesh are intrinsically evil; but that since, unfortunately, conception cannot take place without intercourse, sexual relations within marriage are not sinful, provided they are undertaken purely for the purpose of procreation—and provided, apparently, that the partners do not enjoy them. Thus Augustine wrote that 'sexual intercourse in marriage should not be a matter of mere desire but of necessary duty. . . . The union of the marriage bed is not in itself sin, when it is contracted with the intention of producing children; because the prurient activity which plays the king in the foul indulgences of lasciviousness . . . in the indispensable duties of the marriage bed exhibits the docility of the slave.' However, Augustine added, since it is now possible to increase the number of Christians by conversion as well as by breeding, complete abstinence is probably the ideal.

Throughout the whole of Augustine's treatise *On Marriage and Concupiscence*[7] from which the above quotations are taken (Book I Chaps. 9, 13, 14), there is scarcely a mention of love. Marriage is treated simply as a tolerated safety-valve for undesirable bodily urges, and as a means of producing children. The Augustinian view of sex prevailed throughout and beyond the Dark Ages. In the sixth century Pope Gregory the Great in his *Pastoral Care* proclaimed that 'The married must be admonished to bear in mind that they are united in wedlock for the purpose of procreation. . . . Wherefore, it is necessary that they should efface by frequent prayer what they befoul in the fair form of intercourse by the admixture of pleasure.'[8] Centuries later the doctrine had been but slightly modified. In the twelfth century even Abelard, towards the end of his heartrending correspondence with Heloise after their separation, told her that though sex within marriage could sometimes be regarded 'with indulgence' even when procreation was not its object, this was so only if the couple sought intercourse 'as a remedy for their incontinence and not for pleasure and the delight of the flesh in the manner of beasts.'[9] *Tantum religio potuit suadere malorum.*

A further development of the Augustinian doctrine was the view that we are all tainted with original sin as the result of our carnal conception (as Pope Innocent III nicely put it 'heat and foul concupiscence befoul and corrupt the conceived seeds'[10]), but that the taint can be removed by baptism. It was held at first that Jesus alone, being born of a virgin, was free from this primal stain. But, later, disturbing problems arose regarding the virgin herself. Was it conceivable that the Mother of God bore the taint of original sin? This problem troubled the Church for centuries, but in 1854 Pope Pius IX removed all uncertainties by proclaiming the dogma of the Immaculate Conception. This doctrine (not to be confused with the Virgin Birth) states that Mary, though not miraculously born, was miraculously cleansed from original sin at the moment of her conception.

There had also been difficulties about Jesus' brothers and sisters. By the sixth century Mary was being worshipped as a minor divinity, and it was felt to be unthinkable that the Queen of Heaven should have so demeaned herself on earth as to have had sexual relations

with her husband. Yet the New Testament is unambiguous. Matthew (i, 25) speaks of Jesus as Mary's 'first-born
son'; Paul (Galatians i, 19) refers to James as 'the brother
of our Lord'; and Matthew describes how, when Jesus
revisited his native Galilee, the people said 'Is not this the
carpenter's son? Is not his mother called Mary? And his
brethren, James and Joses and Simon and Judas, and his
sisters, are they not all with us?' (Matt. xiii, 55–6. Also
Mark vi, 3). But Catholic theologians disposed of this
problem by a stroke of the pen. They simply asserted that
the Greek word *adelphos*, which means and always has
meant nothing but 'brother', must be here understood to
mean 'cousin'; or alternatively that James, Joses and the
rest were children of Joseph by a former marriage.*

But to return to the Fathers of the Church—who, in
the words of Pope Pius XII (Encyclical *Sacra Virginitas*,
1954) 'have abundantly illustrated the numerous advan-
tages for advancement in spiritual life which derive from
a complete renouncement of all sexual pleasure'. St
Augustine, as has already been stated, held that sex
relations were permissible within marriage provided that
their sole aim was procreation. But some of the earlier
Fathers were as much opposed to parenthood as to
sex.

The reason put forward for this was that the impending
end of the world would be preceded by a time of tribula-
tion (cf. Mark xiii, 8–25), and that Christians would be in
a better position to surmount the ordeals ahead if they

---

* The doctrine of the lifelong virginity of Mary, though now
abandoned by most Protestants, is still an article of faith with the
Catholic Church. Thus when, in the 1950s, the BBC produced a
play showing Mary and Joseph in middle age surrounded by their
children, there were indignant protests from the hierarchy and
embarrassed apologies from the Corporation.

were unhampered by family ties. This is an understandable if not a very appealing attitude; but the sick revulsion of the Fathers from the physical aspects of sex and procreation ('swollen breasts and nauseating wombs and whimpering infants', as Tertullian gracefully put it[11]) doubtless stemmed more from their own repressions than from any considerations of prudence.

If first marriages were deplored, second marriages were regarded with peculiar horror. In a letter to a protégée, Furia, who was contemplating this step, St Jerome drew a parallel, almost unquotable even in this uninhibited age, between a widow who remarries and a dog that returns to its vomit.[12]

To be dedicated as a virgin in childhood was, in the view of the Fathers, the ideal destiny for a young girl, and in a letter to a mother, Laeta, whose daughter was thus destined, Jerome prescribed the régime to be adopted.

Let her never appear in public without you. . . . Let no youth or curled dandy ogle her. Let our little virgin never stir a finger's breadth from her mother when she attends a vigil or an all-night service. . . . Let her choose as companion not a spruce, handsome girl able to warble sweet songs in liquid notes, but one grave and pale, carelessly dressed and inclined to melancholy. Set before her as a pattern some aged virgin of approved faith, character and chastity, one who may instruct her by word, and by example, accustom her to rise from her bed at night for prayer and psalm singing, to chant hymns in the morning, at the third, sixth and ninth hour. . . . So let the day pass, and so let the night find her still labouring. Let reading follow prayer and prayer follow reading. The time will seem short when it is occupied with such a diversity of tasks. . . . I disapprove altogether of baths in the case of a full-grown virgin. She ought to blush at herself and be unable to look at her own nakedness. If she mortifies and enslaves her body by vigils and fasting, if she desires to quench the flame of lust and to check the hot desires of youth by a cold chastity, if she hastens to spoil her natural beauty by a deliberate squalor, why should she rouse a sleeping fire by the incentive of baths?[13]

In parenthesis—the belief that personal hygiene was an obstacle to virtue seems to have been universal among the Fathers. In another letter Jerome wrote that 'he who has once washed in Christ has no need to wash again',[14] and he recounted of the saintly Paula (cf. p. 70) that when, as head of a convent, 'she chanced to notice any sister too attentive to her dress, she reproved her for her error with knitted brows and severe looks, saying: "A clean body and a clean dress mean an unclean soul".'[15] Many other examples are quoted by Lecky,[16] among them that of St Antony, the subject of a famous painting by Pieter Breughel, of whom Athanasius related with enthusiasm that he had never, to extreme old age, been guilty of washing his feet.*

---

* Even professional Christians, it would seem, are ill-informed on this subject. Thus our leading popular apologist, Donald Soper (now Lord Soper) wrote indignantly in his book *Popular Fallacies about the Christian Faith* (1938), 'Some years ago a well-known atheist declared that primitive Christianity was opposed to the ordinary habits of personal cleanliness, and that Christians were encouraged not to wash, as such habits did not conduce to the Glory of God. To say that this is a ludicrous caricature is to understate the case, but . . . it persists to this day, despite the irrefutable evidence that can easily be found to prove it a falsehood' (p. 12). He does not say where the 'irrefutable evidence' is to be found.

It is a matter of speculation how far the Fathers themselves lived up to the ideals of chastity they recommended to women. But there can be no doubt that in later centuries outraged nature, in Gibbon's phrase, frequently claimed her rights, and clerical celibacy became no more than nominal. To quote Lecky:

> It is a popular illusion, which is especially common among writers who have little direct knowledge of the middle ages, that the atrocious immorality of the monasteries in the century before the Reformation was a new fact, and that the ages when the faith of men was undisturbed were ages of great moral purity. In fact, it appears, from the uniform testimony of the ecclesiastical writers, that ecclesiastical immorality in the eighth and three following centuries was little if at all less outrageous than in any other period, while the Papacy, during almost the whole of the tenth century, was held by men of infamous lives. . . . An Italian bishop of the tenth century epigrammatically described the morals of his time when he declared that if he were to enforce the canons against unchaste people administering ecclesiastical rites, no-one would be left in the church except the boys; and if he were to observe the canons against bastards, these also must be excluded.[17]

But to return to the question of women. Admittedly, those who say that women's position was improved by Christianity are not usually basing their claim on the Dark Ages. What they commonly have in mind is the courtly world of the Middle Ages—that fantastic period of chivalry and romance when noble women were courted and adored at a distance in a rarefied atmosphere untainted by sensuality. It is a far more attractive ethos than the squalid asceticism of the Fathers. But there is still, surely, a hint of perversion about it. In the third of his TV talks on Civilization, entitled *Romance and Reality*, Sir Kenneth Clark (now Lord Clark) dealt with this period, and he said:

> Of the two or three faculties that have been added to the European mind since the civilization of Greece and Rome, none seems to me stranger and more inexplicable than the sentiment of ideal or courtly love. It was entirely unknown to antiquity. Passion, yes; desire, yes of course; steady affection, yes. But this state of utter subjection to the will of an almost unapproachable woman; this belief that no sacrifice was too great, that a whole lifetime might properly be spent in paying court to some exacting lady or suffering on her behalf— this would have seemed to the Romans or to the Vikings not only absurd but unbelievable; and yet for hundreds of years it passed unquestioned.[18]

Sir Kenneth then went on to speculate on how the cult of ideal love arose, and made the interesting suggestion that a major cause may have been the cult of the virgin, grafted, so to speak, on to the Saracen ideals of chivalry that had spread northwards from Spain.

Whatever its origin, it must be realized that the world of chivalry, as depicted in art and literature, is largely a dream world. There was another side to the picture. The exquisite medieval ladies who were the subject of courtly love-poems had commonly been forced into loveless marriages of convenience by their families, and were thereafter beaten by their husbands if they were insufficiently obedient, and locked into iron chastity-belts when their 'lords' were away from home. The contrast is vividly brought out in a medieval manual of female deportment by a certain Knight of the Tower of Landry. This knight was a widower, and he wrote his book mainly for the edification of his three young daughters—believing, as he said, that 'at the beginning a man ought to learn his daughters with good examples'. Written originally about 1370, the book proved so successful that it continued to be widely read right up to the sixteenth century. It begins exquisitely:

In the year of the incarnation of our Lord 1371 as I was in a garden, all heavy and full of thought, in the shadow, about the end of the month of April, but a little I rejoiced me of the melody and song of the wild birds; they sang there in their languages, as the Thrustill, the thrush, the nightingale, and other birds, the which were full of mirth and joy; and their sweet song made my heart to lighten, and made me to think of the time that is passed of my youth, how love in great distress had held me, and how I was in her service many times full of sorrow and gladness, as many lovers be. But my sorrow was healed, and my service well beset and quit, for he gave me a fair wife, and . . . that was both fair and good, which had knowledge of all honour, all good, and fair maintaining, and of all good she was bell and the flower; and I delighted me so much in her that I made for her love songs, ballads, roundels, virelays, and divers new things in the best wise that I could. But death, that on all maketh war, took her from me, the which hath made me have many a sorrowful thought and great heaviness. And so it is more than twenty year that I have been for her full of great sorrow. For a true lover's heart forgetteth never the woman that once he hath truly loved.

Here, one feels, is medieval Christian chivalry at its best. But there is a disconcerting change of tone when the knight proceeds to his 'good examples', which consist in large part of cautionary tales about the treatment to be expected by wives who are disobedient, unfaithful or too fond of personal adornment. He relates, for example, what happened to a wife who engaged in the (admittedly heinous) practice of disparaging her husband before others.

And he, that was angry of her governance, smote her with his fist down to the earth; and then with his foot he struck her in the visage and brake her nose, and all her life after she had her nose crooked, the which shent and disfigured her visage after, that she might not for shame show her visage, it was so foul blemished. (xviii)

Again, the knight describes how three merchants, in the manner of Petruchio and his friends in the last act of *The Taming of the Shrew*, laid a wager as to whose wife was the most obedient. The first ordered his wife to jump into a basin. She demanded to know why, and refused to comply until she was given a reason. 'So her husband up with his fist, and gave her two or three great strokes.' The second wife was equally obdurate, and her husband 'took a staff and all to-beat her.' The third obeyed, and won her husband the wager. 'And so,' comments the knight, 'ought every good woman do the commandment of her husband, be it evil or well, for if he bid her thing that she ought not to do, it is his shame.' (xix)

Wives who are unfaithful can expect more drastic

treatment, and for the edification of his 'tender daughters' the knight describes in rather pungent detail what happened to a woman and a monk who were caught *in flagrante delicto*.

> Daughters, I would ye knew an example of a lady that left her lord, the which was a goodly knight, and went away with a monk. And so her brothers went after, and sought her so long till they found her and the monk lying together. And they took a knife, and cut away the monk's stones, and cast them in despite at her visage, and made her eat them. And after they took a great sack, and put her and the monk therein, with many great stones with them, and cast them into the river, and drowned them, and thus they made their end of that foul sin that they were in; for gladly evil life hath evil end. (liv)

The knight's attitudes seem entirely typical of his age, except in the one respect that his romantic feelings were directed towards his wife. Courtly love in the Middle Ages was seldom connubial. Medieval marriages were almost entirely a matter of property, arranged by hard bargaining between the families with no consideration for the feelings of the couple concerned. This side of medieval life is well illustrated in the Paston Letters—a collection of over a thousand letters exchanged between the members of a well-to-do squire's family in the fifteenth century. To take what is admittedly one of the more extreme cases, the letters describe how the squire's wife, Agnes Paston, determined to marry her daughter Elizabeth, aged about twenty, to one Stephen Scrope, a wealthy widower in his fifties who was disfigured by some disease. Elizabeth refused: and her mother kept her confined in the house where 'she has for the most part been beaten once in the week or twice, sometimes twice in one day, and her head broken in two or three places',[19] The unhappy girl at length gave way and agreed to the marriage, but fortunately the arrangements later broke down, for reasons which are not fully revealed in the letters.

The Pastons lived about a century later than the Knight of the Tower, but it is clear from their correspondence that wife-beating was still a normal occurrence. Thus one letter[20] describes how a man, fined for chastising a villein of John Paston over whom he had no legal authority, indignantly wondered what the world was coming to and opined that before long a man might not even be allowed to beat his own wife. That day did indeed come, but not for some two centuries. It was not until the reign of Charles II that assault and battery became illegal within marriage as well as outside it.

So far nothing has been said about the property rights of women in Christianized Europe. It will be remembered that in pagan Rome under the Empire women inherited their share of their father's wealth and retained control of their inheritance when they married. In the first centuries after the conversion of Rome women could not inherit at all, though they later acquired that right in the absence of a male heir. But in the feudal period a woman who inherited any considerable amount of property, either from a deceased husband or from her father, was promptly married off by the king or her feudal lord to a husband of his choice, to whom the whole of her property passed. Until the end of the nineteenth century the law decreed that, with the possible exception of a few 'chattels', a wife could own no property in her own right. Thus in

The Merchant of Venice Shakespeare's Portia, 'richly left'
by her father, says to Bassanio on their betrothal:

> Myself, and what is mine, to you and yours
> Is now converted: but now I was the lord
> Of this fair mansion, master of my servants,
> Queen o'er myself; and even now, but now
> This house, these servants, and this same myself
> Are yours my lord: I give them with this ring.
>   (Act III, scene 2)

The question of a wife's earnings did not arise until a
later period of history. But when married women began
to take paid employment, their earnings, like their
property, belonged unreservedly to their husbands. Thus
if the wife of an unemployable drunkard went out to
work to support her children, her husband would be
entirely within his legal rights in confiscating her earnings
and spending them on drink. This situation was ended in
England in 1870, when the Married Women's Property
Act emancipated a wife's earnings from her husband's
control. In 1882 the same principles were applied to all
property. Thus, to quote Westermarck, 'It has taken
nearly 2000 years for the married woman to get back that
personal independence which she enjoyed under the later
Roman law, but lost through the influence which
Christianity exercised on European legislation. And it
may be truly said that she has regained it, not by the aid
of the Churches, but despite their opposition.'[21]

SEVENTEEN

SLAVERY

It is not uncommon, when Periclean Athens is being eulogized, for someone to deny its claim to greatness on the ground that it was based on slavery. The statement is of course true in a sense; but it is highly misleading if Athenian slavery is thought of as analogous to negro slavery. A few facts about Athenian slavery may help to bring out the difference.

The number of slaves in Athens in the fourth century BC is estimated at about 20,000, or one to every three adult free persons. The great majority of these slaves were, in effect, prisoners of war—some taken directly by the Athenians, others the victims of war between 'barbarian' tribes, who had been sold into slavery by the conquerors. Their freedom was limited, as is that of prisoners of war everywhere. But they were not deprived of human dignity or treated as chattels. They could own property and earn money, and a slave with ability could usually save enough in a few years to purchase his freedom. Slaves, like other resident aliens, could not hold public office or vote in the Assembly, but apart from this there was almost no occupation or activity open to Athenians in which slaves did not also engage, often side by side with free men.

A valuable corrective to mistaken ideas about Athenian slavery is provided by *Slavery in Classical Antiquity*—a collection of articles by leading historical and classical

scholars, reprinted from various journals and edited by
M. I. Finley, Professor of Ancient History at Cambridge.
Two quotations follow.

Western scholars bring with them fixations upon
[this] subject which derive from negro slavery. In
[studying Greek slavery] therefore, we must first
discard ... all of the canalized habits of thought upon
slavery which we moderns carry about with us. ...
Two peculiarities of Greek city-state slavery distinguish
it ... from any other system of bondage known to me.
The first is ... the custom of purchase by the city-
state of slaves who were employed in its bureaucratic
services. ... The Romans used *servi publici* ... upon a
wide scale. But where else than in Greece will one find
a purchased group of public slaves used as a police
force, armed, and with powers of arresting the free?
... The second peculiarity is the existence of benefit
clubs called *eranoi*. ... One of these types of club
advanced money to slaves which they, in turn, used for
the purchase of their freedom.[1]

The efficient, skilled, reliable slave could look forward
to managerial status. In the cities, in particular, he
could often achieve a curious sort of quasi-indepen-
dence, living and working on his own, paying a kind
of rental to his owner, and accumulating earnings with
which, ultimately, to purchase his freedom. Manumission was, of course, the greatest incentive of all.[2]

Finally, a revealing sidelight on Athenian slavery is
provided in a pamphlet written by an indignant oligarch
of the fifth century BC, who considered that slaves in his
day were being ridiculously over-indulged. They will
not, he protested, make way for you in the street, and it is

10

forbidden to strike them—though this is perhaps just as
well, as otherwise one might strike an Athenian by mistake, since there is nothing in dress or bearing to distinguish a slave from a free man. How different, he sighed
regretfully, from Sparta, where a slave is afraid of you.[3]

The Romans were traditionally less humane than the
Greeks (as Michael Grant remarks, it was not for nothing
that the axe and the rods were the emblems of Roman
authority), and in the later years of the republic slaves were
often treated with revolting cruelty. But their position
improved steadily under the Emperors, and the situation
around the time of Trajan has been thus described by an
Oxford classicist, J. D. Balsdon.

> We think of Roman slavery, perhaps, in too heavily
> loaded and emotional terms, and forget two things:
> first, that there was a greater potential of varied genius
> among slaves (a great many of whom came from the
> Greek-speaking East) than in any other section of the
> Roman community and, secondly, that in a large, and
> particularly, in the Empire, in the imperial, household
> a quick and bright young slave had the possibility of
> a really exciting future.... Apart from technical
> specialists of all kinds, there was always an extensive
> need in public service, in the imperial household and
> in commercial life for linguists ... for shorthand
> writers (*notarii*), for clerks and accountants and, in
> private life, for slaves of good literary education....
> With the need of such specialists in view, two great
> imperial training schools (*paedagogia*) for slave-boys
> were set up in Rome.... Similar schools for the
> training of young slaves were established by wealthy
> individuals with large slave households, and it has been
> conjectured that the younger Pliny had such an
> establishment at his Laurentine villa.

Though there were many who lived and died as slaves, the intelligent and enterprising slave lived in the hope of eventual manumission. This was something that he might buy with part or the whole of his *peculium*, capital which he acquired if he was set up in business of any sort, which by law was the master's property but in practice was treated as belonging to the slave, or he might receive freedom without payment, by gift of his master.[4]

There is, of course, another side to the picture. Slaves who had not the good fortune to serve in the imperial household, or under an enlightened master like Pliny, were still sometimes treated with appalling cruelty. Ancient Rome, like all other communities, had its quota of perverts and sadists, and the unfortunate slaves, who had at first no legal protection, were their natural victims. But such cruelty was execrated by the people in general: Seneca, writing around the middle of the first century AD, described how 'Cruel masters are pointed at with scorn throughout the whole city, and are hated and loathed.'[5] By the second century cruelty to slaves was not merely execrated but punishable by law—under Hadrian a Roman matron, one Umbricia, was banished for five years for this cause. Further, officers were appointed in all the provinces to hear the complaints of slaves, and slaves acquired the right, in certain circumstances, to bring actions at law against their masters.

This improvement was not the result of Christian teaching; it was due primarily to the Stoic doctrine of the brotherhood of man, though there was also the less lofty motive that when the Roman Empire ceased to expand the supply of prisoners of war fell off, and slaves became more valued possessions. But the spread of Christianity produced a still further improvement, though the Church did not condemn slavery as such—its belief that all men were equal before God did not imply that they should be treated as equals in the human community. The suggestion rather was that differences of status in this world should be accepted without question since *sub specie aeternitatis* they were meaningless. As Paul put it 'Let every man abide in the same calling wherein he was called. . . . For he that is called in the Lord, being a servant, is the Lord's freeman: likewise also he that is called, being free, is Christ's servant' (I Cor. vii, 20, 22). (The Greek word *doulos*, meaning a slave, is wrongly translated in the Authorized Version as 'servant'). Again, in the fourth century Lactantius wrote—

Some one will say, Are there not among you some poor, and others rich; some slaves and others masters? Is there not some difference between individuals? There is none; nor is there any other cause why we mutually bestow upon each other the name of brethren, except that we believe ourselves to be equal. For since we measure all human things not by the body, but by the spirit, although the condition of bodies is different, yet we have no slaves, but we both regard and speak of them as brothers in spirit, in religion as fellow-slaves.[6]

Slaves could be pardoned for regarding this rather elusive status as a poor substitute for freedom. But though the Church showed no great zeal for liberating slaves (and indeed employed large numbers of them in the monasteries) it undoubtedly did something to alleviate their lot. It urged Christian masters to treat their slaves kindly, particularly if the slaves themselves were Christians, and it encouraged manumission up to a point—though, paradoxically, monastic slaves were among the last to be released, apparently on the ground that such slaves did not belong to the individual monastery but to the Church, and that the monastery had no right to alienate corporate property.

In the event, slavery lasted in Europe for about 800 years after Constantine, and its final disappearance, or rather its transformation into serfdom, was due to economic rather than religious causes. The Roman *colonus*, who was the forerunner of the medieval serf, held land on lease, paying a fixed proportion of the produce to the owner of the estate, and giving a fixed amount of labour on that part of the estate which the owner retained. He was permanently attached to the estate and could not marry outside it. This system, with minor modifications, developed into serfdom or villeinage, which was basic to the feudal system in Europe and which survived in 'Holy Russia' until the nineteenth century.

Negro Slavery

An entirely new form of slavery came into being in the fifteenth century, when the European countries began their overseas explorations and colonizing. Prosperity in the colonies called for the large-scale production of exportable crops such as cotton, rice and sugar, and this in turn required an abundance of cheap labour which was not readily obtainable in the colonies themselves. So the Europeans turned to the African negro as an answer to their labour problem, and for nearly four centuries the African continent was raided to supply the demand for labour in the New World.

The principal slave-trading country was England,

which held the monopoly of supply not only for her own American colonies but, as a result of Marlborough's victories in Spain, for the Spanish-American colonies also. By 1800 about six-sevenths of all the slaves from Africa were transported in ships coming from the port of Liverpool alone.

It is unnecessary to enlarge on the horrors of the African slave trade, which today are sufficiently well known. The point that concerns us here is that, in the words of H. A. L. Fisher, 'It is a terrible commentary on Christian civilization that the longest period of slave-raiding known to history was initiated by the action of Spain and Portugal, France, Holland and Britain, after the Christian faith had for more than a thousand years been the established religion of Europe.'[7] But the Christian churches, in general, accept no responsibility and express no contrition for this appalling stain on their record. Instead they blandly congratulate themselves on the fact that eventually, after nearly four centuries, the slave trade was abolished; and they claim, with the slenderest justification, that they themselves were responsible for its abolition.

If this presumptuous claim is to be defended, it can only be by confining attention to the abolitionist movement in England, to the exclusion of France and America, and by ignoring all English abolitionists who were not Christians. To most people in Britain, of course, the abolitionist movement means William Wilberforce and almost nobody else; and Wilberforce, as everyone knows, was a Christian, though not everyone knows that he was a sceptic until his mid-twenties, whereas his opposition to the slave trade dated from his schooldays. But in any case Wilberforce was not the originator of the abolitionist movement in England. This honour belongs to the

Quakers—that numerically insignificant splinter-group which, by abandoning the other-worldliness of orthodox Christianity and devoting itself to improving the quality of human life in this world, has done more for humanity than all the Christian churches together.

In 1729 the Quakers in England declared slavery to be 'not a commendable or allowed practice', and in 1761 they excluded from the Society of Friends all persons who were involved in the slave trade. When in 1787 the Society for the Abolition of the Slave Trade was formed under the presidency of Granville Sharp, nine of its twelve members were Quakers. Wilberforce was not one of the original twelve, but he later became acknowledged leader of the abolitionist movement and its first parliamentary spokesman—a task for which he was ideally suited, since he was well-to-do, well-connected and had many influential friends, including William Pitt, the Prime Minister, who fully shared his views on the iniquity of slavery. In 1789 Wilberforce made the first cautious move in Parliament by proposing, and successfully carrying, a motion that the Privy Council should investigate the question of the slave trade. In 1792 he introduced a more radical motion 'for leave to bring in a Bill to prevent the further importation of slaves into the British islands in the West Indies', which was narrowly defeated despite a magnificent speech by Pitt. Nine months later Britain and France were at war, which inevitably absorbed most of Pitt's time and energy, so that the question of the slave trade fell into the background. But in 1807 Pitt's successor, Charles James Fox, who had always been strongly opposed to the slave trade, successfully carried a motion for its abolition; and in 1833 slavery itself was abolished, and the slaves were freed.

Throughout the campaign Wilberforce's chief allies were Quakers, dissenters and sceptics. He received almost no support from the Established Church, whose attitude he described as 'disgracefully lukewarm'.[8] To quote G. M. Trevelyan, 'Wilberforce confessed with chagrin that the "high and dry" conservative party then prevalent among the Church clergy obstructed the anti-slavery cause or were at best indifferent, while nonconformists and godless reformers proved his staunchest allies.'[9] The 'godless reformers' included Jeremy Bentham, Lord Brougham and, above all, Pitt and Fox, who were both unbelievers though the fact is not often mentioned. However, it is fair to say that the motive force of the abolitionist movement in England was largely, though by no means wholly, religious. The same cannot be said of France and America, where the inspiration came from the secular humanitarianism of the Enlightenment.

The first society formed for the abolition, not only of the slave trade but of slavery itself, was the *Société des Amis des Noirs*, founded in 1788. Its president was Condorcet, and its members included many leading figures of the Revolution; Mirabeau was an active supporter. In the United States Benjamin Franklin, Washington, Jefferson and John Quincey Adams, who were among the most prominent early critics of slavery, were freethinkers or deists; while Abraham Lincoln, in the words of his legal partner Stuart Herndon, 'went farther against Christian beliefs and doctrines and principles than any man I ever heard'.[10]

In England, as Wilberforce said, the Established Church was 'shamefully lukewarm' about abolition. In America the Churches—with the honourable exception, once

again, of the Quakers—were actively hostile. Their opposition provides a striking example of the limitations of a
purely legalistic and authoritarian morality. To the
orthodox Christian at the time, the most important moral
question posed by slavery was not whether it caused
intolerable human suffering and degradation, but whether
or not the Bible forebade it. And clearly the Bible did
not: the Old Testament sanctions slavery (cf. Leviticus
xxv, 44–6); the Gospels contain no condemnation of it;
and St Paul told slaves to obey their masters (Coloss. iii,
22), and sent a runaway slave back to his owner
(Philemon). So it was concluded that slavery cannot be
wrong, and any lingering scruples were dispelled by the
comforting thought that the slaves were being brought
into contact with a higher civilization, and offered the
priceless benefit of Christian baptism.

In their defence of slavery, the Churches repeatedly
used the argument that it was sanctioned by scripture.
Thus the South Carolina Methodist Conference of 1836
declared that 'the Holy Scriptures, so far from giving any
countenance to (the) delusion (of abolitionism) do un-
equivocally authorize the relation of master and slave'.[11]
In the same year, Charles Hodge, editor of the journal of
the Theological Seminary at Princeton, wrote: 'The
assumption that slaveholding is itself a crime . . . is an
error fraught with evil consequences. It not merely brings
its advocates into conflict with the scriptures, but it does
much to retard the progress of freedom: it embitters and
divides the members of the community, and it distracts
the Christian Church.'[12] Two years later Hodge wrote
that abolitionists 'consider their own light as more sure
than the word set down in scripture'.[12]

Slavery in America was finally abolished in 1865; at the

time of writing there are still negroes alive whose grand-
fathers were slaves. But it must not be thought that this
was the end of slavery in the Christian world, for in the
Christian state of Abyssinia slavery was not abolished
until 1942. It is hardly a record of which Christianity can
be proud.

PART III

CHRISTIANITY TODAY

EIGHTEEN

INTRODUCTION

Any Christians who may have read to this point may by
now be wishing that they could confront me in argument.
What conceivably is the point, they may wish to ask, of
retailing so may crimes and horrors in your earlier
chapters? None of them has any relevance to Christianity
today. Why not take a cool look at Christianity as it is
now, instead of dragging up a past that is better forgotten?

But there are good reasons for dragging up the past.
One of the principal arguments used by those who want
at all costs to preserve Christianity is to say that it has been
an immense force for good throughout history and is the
source of all that is best in our civilization. I have tried in
the preceding chapters to show that this view is mistaken;
and it is impossible to do this without mentioning a
number of facts of which Christians would prefer to be
ignorant. To quote Professor William Empson:

> Many good people still believe that support for
> Christianity is a public duty, however absurd it feels,
> because other people (though not themselves) cannot
> be made good without it. A great deal of whitewashing
> still hides from them that, until there were enough
> influential and well-intentioned sceptics about, the
> Christians could not be prevented from behaving with
> monstrous wickedness. It remains a tribute to the
> stamina of European civilization that the religion could
> not corrupt us even more than it did, and by this time

we seem pretty well inoculated against its more virulent forms. But it is not sensible to talk about Christianity so cosily as is now usual, ignoring its theoretical evil, ignoring its consequent use of rack, boot, thumbscrew and slow fire.[1]

This is not to deny, of course, that Christianity has also done some good; it would be astonishing if it had not, in view of the fact that for nearly a thousand years the Church was the most powerful institution in Europe. But in assessing Christianity's record it is necessary to weigh the good against the evil; whereas, to quote Bradlaugh, 'It is customary, in controversy, for those advocating the claims of Christianity to include all good done by men in nominally Christian countries as if such good were the result of Christianity, while they contend that the evil which exists prevails in spite of Christianity.'[2]

As an example of this technique I quote from Basil Willey, formerly Professor of English Literature at Cambridge. He wrote:

This simple yet lofty code of ethics, enriched by elements from pagan antiquity . . . and from chivalry . . . was the source of every good and noble thing produced by European civilization: hospitals, universities, schools, churches, help for the oppressed, the aged and the sick, social justice, the democratic ideals of liberty, equality and fraternity, liberation of slaves, respect for other people's happiness and property, regard for the sanctity of marriage and all the family relationships. True, it also produced some ugly things, such as persecutions, the Inquisition and the Wars of Religion; but these were the defects of its virtues.[3]

Such distortions of history are to be expected from the pulpit, but it is surprising to find them in the writings of a distinguished literary scholar. It is unnecessary to examine Professor Willey's claims in detail, or to comment on the staggering complacency of his final sentence. But in his list of the alleged achievements of Christianity there are two items—namely those relating to education and the care of the sick and aged—for which a case can at least be argued, so brief reference must be made to them here, though education will be discussed more fully in the final chapter.

The medieval Church, powerful and by this time immensely wealthy, was the accepted authority on, and held the primary responsibility for, all matters classed as 'spiritual'—a term that was interpreted extremely widely, and included many departments of life that are now the concern of the secular authorities. Among these were education and the care of the sick; so it can justly be claimed that in medieval Europe such schools and hospitals as existed were financed and controlled by the Church. But it is preposterous to suggest that these institutions owed their existence to Christianity. There had been schools and hospitals in pagan Greece and Rome, and throughout the Roman Empire. In 335, however, all the pagan hospitals in Europe were closed by the Emperor Constantine. Thereafter they were gradually replaced by Christian institutions, but the Church's contempt for the body, and its belief in the salutary effects of suffering, did not conduce to much enthusiasm for the study and practice of healing, and by the Middle Ages the hospitals, no less than the schools and universities, of Christendom were far inferior to those in the Muslim world.

The technique we have been discussing—that of claiming that everything good is by definition Christian —is applied to people as well as to institutions. Any man or woman who has worked selflessly for humanity is commonly said to have been inspired by Christian conviction; and if the individual in question happens not to have been a Christian, and some troublesome Humanist points this out, the answer frequently given is that he must have been 'really' a Christian, otherwise he would not have done so much good.

Two of the greatest benefactors to humanity in the nineteenth century were Abraham Lincoln (cf. p. 142) and Florence Nightingale. But how many people know that they were both non-Christians? Florence Nightingale in particular is repeatedly cited as a supreme example of the Christian spirit in action,* but she was in fact, like Voltaire and Tom Paine, a freethinking deist, whose philosophy of life had far more in common with present-day Scientific Humanism than with Christianity. In her privately printed book *Suggestions for Thought* (which all her friends, with the exception of John Stuart Mill, urged her strongly not to publish) she made many scathing comments on the negative, passive character of Christian ethics, and particularly on its preoccupation, as she put it,

* Thus one of Christianity's most highly-esteemed lay apologists, Professor C. A. Coulson FRS, the distinguished scientist and mathematician, said in a broadcast discussion that 'Florence Nightingale was the person she was for the reason she herself stated, which was that she held certain views about the Christian faith very strongly' (*Listener*, 17 July 1958). The wording is somewhat ambiguous, but Professor Coulson was evidently not referring simply to Florence Nightingale's views *about* Christianity: he was claiming that she was a believing Christian, as is clear from the fact that he went on immediately to cite William Wilberforce, Lord Shaftesbury and Elizabeth Fry.

with 'smuggling a man selfishly into heaven instead of setting him actively to regenerate the earth'.[4]

One of the greatest humanitarians of our own century was Fridjhof Nansen. He is now remembered mainly as a Polar explorer, but in the later part of his life, after the First World War, he organized a vast system of repatriation and famine relief and became known as the Conscience of Europe. Reviewing a biography of him written by his daughter, the *Listener* said: 'Nansen help and Nansen passports brought life and hope to tens of thousands. . . . He travelled everywhere ceaselessly pleading for money from tight-fisted governments and organizing relief. To the cause of suffering humanity he literally gave his life. He died, a man of tremendous constitution and vitality, worn out by his labours at the age of sixty-nine.'[5]

Nansen was an outspoken atheist, as is clear both from his own writings and from the biography referred to above. But when, in 1961, the BBC gave an hour-long radio programme in commemoration of Nansen's centenary, the script was so worded that all but the most alert listeners would have derived the impression from it that Nansen was a Christian. I wrote an article in the *Spectator* protesting about this;[6] which evoked the characteristic reply in the correspondence columns that 'it does not matter that Nansen did not believe in God, for he showed by his actions what it was to be a true Christian'.

Disingenuousness and *suppressio veri* that would be roundly condemned in any other context are apparently acceptable in the service of Christianity. And it is to be feared that something more than *suppressio veri* has gone to the production of the many stories about the conversion or deathbed 'repentance' of eminent unbelievers such as

Voltaire, Thomas Paine, Abraham Lincoln and Darwin.
Soon after the publication of the uuexpurgated edition of
Darwin's *Autobiography* there was a lively correspondence
in the *Scotsman* about his alleged conversion, and it is
impossible to resist quoting two letters which, by a happy
juxtaposition, appeared together (8 May 1958). The first,
written in reply to a correspondent who said he could find
no reference to the alleged conversion in any of Darwin's
biographies, ran:

> Sir,—I regret that Mr Broom has been put to the un-
> rewarding task of perusing the biographies of Darwin
> for an account of his conversion. Here is the source of
> the information concerning Darwin's saving change.
>   Lady Hope gave this wonderful story when she
> addressed a large gathering of young men and women
> at the great educational establishment founded by the
> late D. L. Moody at Northfield, near Boston. Dr
> Cameron asked her to write it out for a wider audience
> in his periodical, *The Boston Watchman Examiner*. Other
> magazines in this country have also published the whole
> of Lady Hope's testimony, including *The Reformation
> Review*, *A Message from God* (October 1955), published
> by C. A. Hammond, London, E.C.1, and the *Monthly
> Record of the Free Church of Scotland* (February 1957).

The second came from Darwin's granddaughter, Lady
Barlow:

> Sir,—The correspondence that has arisen in the *Scotsman*
> over Charles Darwin's alleged visit from Lady Hope
> is perpetuating a myth that was authoritatively denied
> in 1922 by those in the best position to judge of its
> truth or falsity.

Charles Darwin's daughter, Mrs Litchfield, wrote to *The Christian* 23 February 1922: 'I was present at his deathbed. Lady Hope was not present during his last illness, or any illness. I believe he never even saw her, but in any case she had no influence over him in any department of thought or belief. He never recanted any of his scientific views, either then or earlier. We think the story of his conversion was fabricated in USA. In most of the versions hymn-singing comes in, and a summer house where the servants and villagers sang hymns to him. There is no such summer house, and no servants or villagers ever sang hymns to him. The whole story has no foundation whatever.'

Mrs Litchfield also wrote in a letter to a correspondent on the same subject (23 March 1922) that she believed that Lady Hope never had any interview with her father. She says that her brother, Sir Francis Darwin, who was living in Down House at that time, was certain that Lady Hope never came to the house.

Charles Darwin was no controversialist, but I think he would approve of this refutation of a false myth, as the editor of *The Christian* said in February 1922, 'in the interest of truth.'

NINETEEN

THE ROMAN CATHOLIC CHURCH

The Roman Catholic Church today has made some reluctant concessions to Galileo and Darwin, but apart from this it still stands much where it did in the Middle Ages. It remains intolerant, authoritarian and other-worldly; and it still teaches a literal belief in hell.

Intolerance

The Catholic Church, believing as it does that it is the One True Church, divinely guaranteed against error, is inevitably and basically intolerant. She has become somewhat less so of late, but in essence her attitude is still that expressed by Pope Pius XI in his famous letter to Cardinal Gasparri of May 1929. 'In a Catholic state liberty of conscience and liberty of discussion are to be understood and practised in accordance with Catholic doctrine and Catholic laws.'

Even this carefully-qualified endorsement of the right of freedom of conscience is a comparatively recent development. In 1832 Pope Gregory XVI condemned as 'insanity' the view that 'the liberty of conscience and of worship is the peculiar (or inalienable) right of every man' (Encyclical *Mirari Vos*). And in April 1948 the official world organ of the Jesuits *Civilta Cattolica* made the following statement:

The Roman Catholic Church, convinced, through its

divine prerogatives, of being the only true church, must demand the right of freedom for herself alone.... Consequently, in a state where the majority of people are Catholic, the Church will require that legal existence be denied to error, and that if religious minorities actually exist they shall have only a *de facto* existence without opportunity to spread their beliefs. ... In some countries, Catholics will be obliged to ask full religious freedom for all, resigned at being forced to cohabitate where they alone should rightfully be allowed to live. But in doing this the Church does not renounce her thesis ... but merely adapts herself to *de facto* conditions, which must be taken into account in practical affairs.[1]

Not all Catholics, or even all Jesuits, approved of this pronouncement, but it was not repudiated by the Vatican and it seemed unlikely that it ever would be—until, under the inspiration of Pope John XXIII, a great wind of change blew through the Church with the calling of the Second Vatican Council. In 1965 this Council issued a Declaration on Religious Freedom which proclaimed:

All men are to be free from coercion, either by individuals or by social groups or by any human power, in such wise that in matters religious no-one is to be forced to act in a manner contrary to his own beliefs. Nor is anyone to be restrained from acting in accordance with his own beliefs, whether privately or publicly, whether alone or in association with others, always within due limits.[2]

To non-Catholics this will seem to grant no more than is obviously reasonable, but coming from the Catholic Church it indicates a notable change of heart, and it seems already to have modified practice in the more intolerant Catholic countries such as Spain. But one must not hope for too much from it. The opening section of the Declaration contains this significant passage:

> Such liberty gives no individual the right to equate truth and falsehood, nor does it mean that he has no obligation to acquire correct ideas of religion or that he can decide on his own whether or not he will serve God, or in what religion and in what manner. The concept of religious liberty leaves intact the Catholic teaching on the one true religion and one true Church of Christ.[3]

We have not, after all, moved so far from Pope Pius XI's letter to Cardinal Gasparri.

The ecumenical movement (essentially a closing of the ranks of the churches against the common menace of Humanism) has been enthusiastically espoused by the Vatican, but this does not mean that it is prepared to co-operate with the other Christian churches on equal terms. To the Catholic Church Christian unity can mean only one thing—the eventual conversion of all the other Christian churches to Catholicism. The Decree on Ecumenism issued by Vatican II makes this clear.

> Our separated brethren, whether considered as individuals or as communities and churches, are not blessed with that unity which Jesus Christ wished to bestow on all those whom He has regenerated. . . . For it is through Christ's Catholic Church alone, which is the all-embracing means of salvation, that the fullness of the means of salvation can be obtained. . . . Little by little, as the obstacles to perfect ecclesiastical communion are

overcome, all Christians will be gathered, in a common celebration of the Eucharist, into that unity of the one and only Church which Christ bestowed on His Church from the beginning.[4]

Non-Catholic supporters of the ecumenical movement will do well to bear this statement in mind.

Authoritarianism

Believing itself to be guaranteed against error in morals as well as in doctrine, the Catholic Church is also of necessity authoritarian. Herein lies the crux of the difference between Christian and Humanist ethics. The Catholic (and the Protestant too, if he is orthodox) believes in universally valid rules of conduct based on supernatural authority. The Humanist does not; for him, the test of the rightness or wrongness of an act is its effect on human well-being. Rules of conduct of course there must be, but on the Humanist view these are not unalterable divine prescriptions, but merely provide a sort of convenient ready-reckoner telling us (for example) that in the great majority of cases human well-being is best served by our telling the truth, keeping our promises, and respecting other people's property. But there are bound to be some exceptional cases where the rule does not apply—no Humanist, for example, would think it wrong to lie to save a friend from the Gestapo.

Thus the Humanist, confronted by a difficult moral choice, tries to estimate the probable consequences for himself and others of the various lines of action open to him. Whereas the Catholic, so to speak, consults the rule-book, and if the rule appears unambiguous the question is settled—considerations of human well-being are beside the point. This attitude often causes great unhappiness in the field of personal relationships, and in a wider context its effects can be disastrous. To take the most obvious example, the Catholic Church forbids its members to practise contraception, and has been doing its utmost to prevent the spread of contraceptive knowledge in the undeveloped countries. The resultant human suffering is, in the Church's eyes, unimportant; God disapproves of contraception and there is no more to be said. This uncompromising belief would seem to derive from Augustine (cf. p. 122) rather than from the Gospels, but if one asks today how the Church can be so sure of God's views on this matter, one is usually told that contraception is 'against Nature' (as though it were not against Nature to shave), and referred, possibly, to the story of Onan in Genesis xxxviii—though the moral of the story would appear to be, not that *coitus interruptus* is sinful, but that it is sinful for a man to refuse to impregnate his brother's widow. And on these ludicrous grounds depends a prohibition which provides a major threat to human development.

Among educated Catholics today there is a growing mood of rebellion against the Church's teaching on contraception, and after the great thaw begun by Vatican II hopes were felt that John XXIII's successor, Pope Paul VI, would announce some relaxation of the Church's prohibitions. So it came as a shock to the Catholic community—and indeed to the whole civilized world—when in 1968 the Encyclical *Humanae Vitae* uncompromisingly reaffirmed the traditional doctrine.

Yet it is difficult to see what else Pope Paul could have done. Since the dogma of Papal Infallibility was proclaimed in 1870, it has been almost impossible for a Pope to repudiate explicitly any pronouncement on faith or morals made by one of his predecessors. The most he can do is to 'reinterpret' it or to suggest that it has been misunderstood. And the statements of Pius XI in the Encyclical *Casti Connubii* (1930) give small scope for either method. He said:

> No reason, however grave, may be put forward by which anything intrinsically against nature may become conformable to nature and morally good. Since, therefore, the conjugal act is designed primarily by nature for the begetting of children, those who in exercising it deliberately frustrate its natural power and purpose sin against nature and commit a deed which is shameful and intrinsically vicious. . . . Any use whatsoever of matrimony exercised in such a way that the act is deliberately frustrated in its natural power to generate life is an offence against the law of God and of nature, and those who indulge in such are branded with the guilt of a grave sin.

The pronouncements against abortion in *Casti Connubii* are no less emphatic, and it is unlikely that the Church will ever come to terms with the present Abortion Act. Short of this, however, the attitude of Catholic spokesmen has become appreciably more humane in recent years. Forty years ago the official attitude was completely ruthless; it held that abortion was illegal to save the mother's life even where it was morally certain that if the pregnancy were allowed to continue the mother and child would both die. In a book published with official Imprimatur in 1947, the doctrine is stated in question-and-answer form.

Q. If it is morally certain that a pregnant mother and her unborn child will both die, if the pregnancy is allowed to take its course, but at the same time, the attending physician is morally certain that he can save the mother's life by removing the inviable foetus, is it lawful for him to do so?

A. No, it is not. Such a removal of the foetus would be direct abortion.[5]

It would be hard to find a more shocking example of the application of a purely legalistic ethic, regardless of human consequences. But the doctrine was defended as late as 1955 and by no less eminent a Catholic than Lady Longford (then Lady Pakenham) who wrote:

We must face a situation where, until medical science has progressed even further than it has today, there will be a few sad rare cases when neither mother nor child can lawfully be saved. In the last resort it is for God to decide who shall live and who shall die, not the doctor or the husband. Nor is premature death the unspeakable horror which the poor pagan would have us believe. . . . If [God] takes us 'before our time' that does not mean it is before His time.[6]

The bereaved husband, and the possible earlier children of the marriage, now left motherless, might find it hard to see the matter in this light. As for the attitude ascribed to the 'poor pagan'—if this patronizing description is meant to apply to the Greeks and Romans, Lady Longford is wide of the mark. These pagans would doubtless have thought it folly to fling away a valuable life to no purpose, but they were far from regarding early death as an 'unspeakable horror' if it was faced in a worthy cause.

Has Lady Longford forgotten the Latin tag, 'Dulce et decorum est pro patria mori', and Simonides's epitaph on the Spartans who fell at Thermopylae?

> Tell Sparta, ye who pass this monument,
> We died for her, and here we rest content.

And has she not read Pericles's funeral oration for the dead of the Peloponnesian war?*

However, the ruthless doctrine proclaimed in the mid-century seems today to have been quietly dropped, and many Catholic doctors are now willing to remove even a 'viable' foetus if this is the only way to save the mother's life. But in so doing they are running counter to *Humanae Vitae* which states that 'directly willed and procured abortion, even if for therapeutic reasons, is to be absolutely excluded'.

---

* A passage from this speech may be quoted:
I shall not, therefore, commiserate with those parents of the dead who stand here. I shall rather try to console them. You know the precariousness of life: and you know that those who have won honour must be deemed fortunate—even though it be an honourable death, like your sons', or an honourable grief, like your own. That the end of happiness and the end of life should come together—this is good fortune. I know that this is a hard saying. The sight of others' happiness will often remind you of what you once enjoyed. . . . But those of you who are still of an age to become parents must be patient in the hope of having more children, who will prevent you from brooding on those that have gone. To Athens these children will be doubly precious—both as filling the empty places, and as a source of security too: for men take more responsible views on public affairs when they have children whose safety is at stake. And to those of you who are now too old to have children, I would say: rejoice that you have been happy for most of your lives, and reflect that what remains is not long: and let the fair fame of the dead be your consolation.

Other-worldliness

The Gospel ethic is of its very nature other-worldly, and the Catholic Church, though it no longer believes that the end of the world is imminent, still holds that our life on earth is important primarily as a preparation for the life to come. In the words of Pope Pius XI 'man is begotten above all, not for this world and for temporal life, but for heaven and eternity'—a statement made in the Encyclical *Casti Connubii*, in the course of condemning the proposals of the eugenicists for preventing the birth of defective children.

This attitude is not confined to the priesthood. To quote some distinguished Catholic laymen: the Director-General of the BBC, Mr Charles Curran, said recently that 'What you do during life has a relevance to what comes afterwards, but it is *after* death that matters.'[7] Mr Christopher Hollis has said that 'It is not the fundamental concern of religion to bring order or civilization to this world. Its fundamental concern is not with life but with death.'[8] Mr Douglas Woodruff, editor of the Catholic weekly *The Tablet*, broadcasting some years ago on the hydrogen bomb, consoled his listeners with the reflection that 'To the Christian the present terrestrial life is the preparation for the real life to which the human race is called';[9] while Mr Evelyn Waugh was even more confident that there was no ground for concern, saying: 'I can see nothing objectionable in the total destruction of the earth, provided it is done, as seems likely, inadvertently'[10] (If it were done deliberately, of course, it would involve the sin of murder, and thus remove the incident from the trivial to the serious category.)

To the other-worldly Catholic, obviously, the prevention of suffering and injustice in this world will appear far less important than it does to the Humanist, for whom this life is all. Indeed, Catholicism today has by no means abandoned the view that suffering is not something to be prevented wherever possible, but to be sought and welcomed on account of the spiritual benefits that it brings. Thus the Dean of the St Louis University Medical School, Father Alphonso Schwitalla, SJ (whom one would not wish to have as one's medical adviser) wrote in 1947 of 'the inexhaustible sublimity of human suffering, the ennobling character of agony'.[11] And the National Catholic Women's Union, which is often used by the hierarchy as a mouthpiece for orthodox utterances, concluded a denunciation of euthanasia by proclaiming that 'suffering is a blessing in disguise'.[12] Even that most enlightened of Popes, John XXIII, as a seminarian, recorded in his diary with the innocent consistency of the young that 'The toothache which seized me suddenly before noon made it an even more well-spent day.'[13]

As a means to the attainment of virtue, poverty and deprivation are considered scarcely less valuable than illness and pain. In the words of Father Martin d'Arcy, SJ, 'Prosperity and comfort are good neither for a nation nor for the individual.'[14] This doctrine has throughout history been highly convenient to the privileged classes, since it has helped to keep the unprivileged resigned to their lot. As Napoleon remarked with his customary realism:

> How can you have order in a state without religion? Society cannot exist without inequality of fortunes, which cannot endure apart from religion. When one man is dying of hunger near another who is ill of surfeit, he cannot resign himself to this difference unless

there is an authority which declares 'God wills it thus: there must be poor and rich in the world: but hereafter and during all eternity the division of things will take place differently.'[15]

It is sad to think how much innocent human happiness has been sacrificed for the sake of an illusory Hereafter. Robert Louis Stevenson in his *Travels with a Donkey* relates a conversation he had with a young Italian monk, destined for a life of silence in the Trappist monastery of Our Lady of the Snows. 'The rule was very hard (the brother said); he would have dearly liked to stay in his own country, Italy—it was well known how beautiful it was, the beautiful Italy; but then there were no Trappists in Italy; and he had a soul to save; and here he was.' Which evoked from Stevenson the comment, 'I am afraid . . . this description of the brother's motives gave me something of a shock. I should have preferred to think he had chosen the life for its own sake, and not for ulterior motives; and this shows how profoundly I was out of sympathy with these good Trappists, even when I was doing my best to sympathize.' He would doubtless have felt the same towards a monk who, questioned recently by Malcolm Muggeridge on TV about his reasons for embracing the monastic life, gave the prompt and embarrassing answer, 'Well, it's the reward isn't it? If I didn't think I was going to get to Heaven I wouldn't be here a week.' Similar considerations of posthumous self-interest may even have been present to Cardinal Heenan when, asked on TV 'What is your chief aim in life?', he replied without hesitation 'to save my immortal soul'.

However, there have recently been signs of a change of heart. Cynics may suggest that it is not unconnected with the challenge of Communism in the more backward Catholic countries; but, whatever the cause, there has recently been a strong movement among younger Catholics towards modifying the Church's traditional other-worldliness, and becoming more concerned with social issues. Indeed there are signs of a split in the Catholic world between the left wingers, who have been influenced by Humanism and who are represented by the new periodical *Slant*, and the conservatives who hold with Arnold Lunn that 'This preoccupation with economics and social problems is evidence of declining belief in the primary mission of the Church: the salvation of souls and the conversion of those who now reject the supernatural.'[16]

Whether the innovators or the conservatives will prevail remains to be seen. But a survey by a Catholic psychologist from London University suggests that, in 1965 at all events, the hold of the traditional attitude was still powerful even among the young. The investigation involved a study of the value-judgments of some three hundred young Catholics, most of them students, who were given a well-known standard test (the Allport-Vernon-Lindzey Study of Values) and another test specially designed to investigate their idea of the Christian ideal. The results may be given in the author's own words.

[Their idea of the Christian ideal] embraces an emphasis on the importance of observing the Church's require-ments for public worship and the observance of rules generally. 'Thou shalt love the Lord thy God', they very properly affirm, but 'thy neighbour as thyself' has an altogether weaker flavour. Just as religion is private and personal . . . so the whole Christian life is seen as ideally little concerned with the wider community. . . . The Good Christian is seen as theocentric, concerned with his own conscience, but not concerned with the personal virtues and social involvements that characterize much of the English way of life at its best. . . . What does emerge very clearly is the essentially private nature of the religion they hold. . . . Clearly they are in no danger of being swept into an heretical over-concern with works.[17]

The book in which this investigation is described is significantly entitled *Out of this World*.

Hell

Non-Catholics today are often incredulous when they are told that the Catholic Church still teaches a literal belief in the fires of hell. So it will be necessary to quote chapter and verse from official and semi-official sources.

The most hair-raising statements are to be found in some of the publications of the Catholic Truth Society, such as the pamphlet, succinctly entitled *Hell*, by the Very Reverend Francis Ripley, Superior of the Catholic Missionary Society and former Director of the Catholic Education Centre in Liverpool. The pamphlet is written in question-and-answer form, and I quote from six items.

Q. What does 'hell' mean?

A. The place and state in which the devils and such human beings as die in enmity with God suffer torment for ever.

Q. Did not some of the Fathers of the Church regard the fire of hell as only figurative?

A. Yes, a few . . . but tradition is overwhelmingly against them. The New Testament describes the punishment of hell as fire no less than thirty times. . . . It is certain that the souls in hell suffer from real, created, physical fire. . . . No Catholic could deny that the fire of hell is real without sinning seriously against faith.

Q. If God knew that certain souls would be damned why did He create them?

A. We have already proved that hell is a fact. It is part of the plan of an infinitely wise, good and powerful God. Therefore it must be the best for his purposes. Who are we to dictate to Him? If we find it hard to reconcile certain facts we must blame our limited knowledge, not God's infinite wisdom.

Q. But how can there be good in creating somebody who is going to be damned?

A. The very fact of his damnation means that he is a terrible witness of the justice of God. . . .

Q. May we pray that the damned will suffer a mitigation of their torment?

A. No. St Thomas Aquinas wrote: 'The damned in hell are outside the bond of charity. . . .'[7]

It may be said that it is not fair to quote from this pamphlet, which, after selling some sixty thousand copies, has recently been allowed to go out of print. But current official statements, though their language is more restrained, are no less emphatic about the reality of hell. The Catholic *Catechism of Christian Doctrine* ('approved by the Archbishops and Bishops of England and Wales and directed to be used in all their dioceses') was reissued in 1971 in a revised form, but there was no change in the two questions and answers about hell, which run:

Q. Where will they go who die in mortal sin?

A. They who die in mortal sin will go to hell for all eternity.

Q. Shall not the wicked also live for ever?
A. The wicked also shall live and be punished for ever
   in the fire of hell.

The Catholic Enquiry Centre has recently issued a series
of leaflets intended to inform non-Catholics about the
faith, and the last of these, *Life for Ever*, issued in 1967
with official Imprimatur, says this about hell.

We cannot question [the reality of hell] when we read
the Bible. Some of the most terrible words in the Bible,
some of the most serious words spoken by Christ, our
Saviour, concern the fate of those who reject God. . . .
In the Sermon on the Mount, Jesus tells us that any
sacrifice or suffering is better than the sentence of everlasting damnation. On other occasions he drove home
the reality of our choice in the parables that he told
us. . . .
   The appalling consequence of rejecting God is quite
clear. The Church of Christ would be failing in its
duty if it did not present this along with the other
teaching of Jesus.

But it is not really necessary to quote from these minor
sources, since a statement is available from the highest
authority of all. In September 1971, at an audience in
Castelgandolfo, Pope Paul said:

Hell is a grim reality even though modern man seems
to be losing sight of the frightful danger of eternal
doom. . . . Today secularization is causing us to lose the
awareness of the frightful danger regarding our future
life, but the Council reminded us of the eschatological
truths affecting us, including the terrible truth of a

possible eternal punishment, called Hell, about which Christ minced no words.[18]

Pope Paul's predecessor, John XXIII does not appear to have said anything about hell during his papacy. But as a seminarian aged nineteen he wrote this in his diary:

The thought of hell terrifies me; I cannot bear it. . . . Yet this is a most certain truth. If I do not fight against my pride, my arrogance and self-esteem, hell awaits me. Oh what a dreadful thought! . . . I must hope this will never happen, but it might. So I must always with fear and trembling work out my own salvation. Meanwhile it will be well constantly to remind myself of hell. . . . If I see fire I must think it is but a painted flame compared with the fire of hell. If I have tooth-ache or a burning thirst, if I tremble with cold or am racked with fever, I must mortify myself: hell is the place of all tortures: in hell we shall burn and glow like coal in the furnace; in hell there will be 'weeping and gnashing of teeth. . . .'

O my most sweet Jesus, listen to this prayer of mine. Send me, I beg you, every sort of illness in this life: confine me to my bed; reduce me to the state of a leper in the woods; load my body with all the most atrocious pains here below, and I will accept all these as a penance for my sins and I will thank you for them, but of your charity do not send me to hell, do not deprive me of your love and of the contemplation of you for all eternity. O Jesus, I say from my heart: 'Here let me burn, here let me be tormented, here do not spare me; but spare me in eternity.'[19]

This was written in 1900: one may hope that young seminarians are not similarly terrorized today. But it is impossible to avoid grave misgivings about what may still be going on in Catholic schools. I remember an occasion when I lectured on Humanism to a group of teachers of varying beliefs, and in the subsequent discussion was gently rebuked by a nun in the audience for exaggeration: Catholic schools, she assured me, did not teach young children about hell. 'At what age then,' I asked, 'do you teach them about it?' 'Not before seven' was the reply.

TWENTY

THE PROTESTANT CHURCH

The Protestant Church today is in a very different position from the Catholic. In the Catholic Church dogma and theology are still of central importance, but liberal Protestantism is now pushing them more and more to one side, so that today the Established Church in England is rapidly becoming little more than a combination of a social club and a charity organization society. In both these capacities it undoubtedly does much good; but the value of its good work must be set against the harm that it does to the cause of clear thought and intellectual integrity.

Today Protestant churchmen, other than fundamentalists, are in an impossible intellectual position. They have ceased to believe most of the things that they are required by the creeds to say they believe; but it is impossible to admit this in so many words, so they devise 'symbolic' interpretations of the troublesome doctrines—interpretations that are usually about as convincing as the earlier 'symbolic' interpretations of the Song of Solomon as a hymn to the perfections of the Church. Or they employ the device known as 're-thinking', which involves, roughly speaking, re-stating traditional doctrines in such a way that they cease to be obviously false by becoming meaningless. In practice the two techniques are often combined.

The best-known practitioner of these methods today is

Dr John Robinson, author of *Honest to God*. But Dr
Robinson, by dissolving the Christian God into something
nebulous which he calls 'depth', 'ultimate reality' or 'the
ground of being', is felt by most Protestants to have gone
too far, and his views have been disowned by many
leading churchmen, including the Archbishop of Canterbury. So I will quote instead from the highest official
source in the Anglican Church—the report, published in
1938, of the Commission on Christian Doctrine appointed
by the Archbishops of Canterbury and York. This report
says:

> Statements affirming particular facts may be found to
> have value as pictorial expressions of spiritual truths,
> even though the supposed facts themselves did not
> actually happen. In that case such statements may be
> called symbolically true. . . . It is not therefore of
> necessity illegitimate to accept and affirm particular
> clauses of the Creeds while understanding them in this
> symbolic sense.[1]

One would naturally like to know which clauses of the
Creeds may be 'understood in this symbolic sense', but
here the Report is not as specific as one could wish.
However, it seems clear that the Ascension and the Last
Judgment, at least, can be regarded as only symbolically
true. The Ascension, of course, has long been a stumbling-
block and one can sympathize with a recent *cri du coeur* in
the *Expository Times*, 'no festival of the church is so hard
on the preacher as Ascensiontide'. To the impartial
reader it seems obvious that the Ascension is a legendary
story, on a par with the similar story (reported, though
sceptically, by Suetonius in *The Twelve Caesars*) that the

soul of the deified Emperor Augustus was seen ascending into heaven from the flames of his funeral pyre. But to the modernist Christian the story of Augustus is pagan superstition, whereas the story of Jesus is 'symbolic truth' —in other words a sort of allegory or parable designed to convey some truth (it is not quite clear what) that is too 'spiritual' to be stated in ordinary language. Thus Bishop F. R. Barry, confronted in 1969 with the unenviable task of composing *The Times* Saturday sermon in Ascension Week, explained that the ascension story is—

> ... not a primitive essay in astrophysics, but the symbol of a creative intuition ... into the abiding significance of Jesus and his place in the destiny of man. It might be called a pictorial presentation of the earliest creed, Jesus is Lord. ... Creed and scripture are saying in their own language that here is something final and decisive, the truth and meaning of man's life and destiny—truth not in a theory but in a person—life in its ultimate quality, that is, God's life.[2]

No amount of careful re-reading can extract much meaning from this passage, but it is clear at least that in the Bishop's opinion the ascension story was not meant to be taken literally. And about this there are two things to be said: first, that the account of the Ascension in Acts (i, 9–11) contains nothing whatever to suggest that it was not meant as a record of fact; and second, that if the writer of the description did indeed mean it to be understood as an allegory, he defeated his own object—for the story has been taken literally throughout almost the whole of the Christian era.

The Last Judgment poses equally intractable problems.

The Gospels represent Jesus as saying quite unambiguously
that he would return to judge the earth within the lifetime of men then living, and that the disciples should live
in daily expectation of this event (cf. p. 35). It was
impossible to say that Jesus was mistaken, and a delicate
matter to suggest that he changed his mind; so the Archbishops' Commission employed the technique described
earlier by Newman as 'guiding the Church through the
channel of no-meaning, between the Scylla and Charybdis
of Aye and No'.[3] They wrote:

> In a literal sense, the *dénouement*, which in the New
> Testament age was expected, did not take place, though
> many scholars have urged ... that there was a real
> Parousia of the glorified Lord in the coming of the
> Spirit. Traditional orthodoxy has tended nevertheless
> to take the scriptural imagery of the Last Things and
> the hoped-for *Parousia* or 'coming' of Christ semi-
> literally, but to explain that the *time* of the coming has
> been postponed. ... Inasmuch, however, as the moral
> urgency of the eschatological message ... is to be found
> largely in the assertion of the *immediate* relation of
> human life, here and now, to its consummation in
> eternity, ... a truer perspective (it may be suggested)
> is to be secured by taking the *imagery* in a symbolical
> sense, but by continuing to affirm, with the New
> Testament, that 'the time is at hand'. The 'time' is, in
> this sense, *always* at hand; and from this point of view
> the spiritual value of the eschatological drama is best
> grasped when it is understood, not as a quasi-literal
> description of a future event, but as a parable of the
> continuous and permanent relation of the perpetually
> imminent eternal order to the process of events in
> time.[4]

It may be felt that this sort of thing, though it provides tempting opportunities for satire, cannot really be said to be morally harmful. But morality has more to do with clear thinking than perhaps is commonly realized. Lord Morley said 'those who tamper with veracity, from whatever motive, are tampering with the vital force of human progress':[5] and modern liberal theology is one long process of tampering with veracity. The effects are particularly harmful when they extend to the classroom, but this is a matter which will be considered in the next and final chapter, which deals with the Church's role in education.

TWENTY ONE

EDUCATION AND THE CHURCHES

As has already been said (p. 149), in the Ages of Faith, when popes and cardinals were more important figures than kings and nobles, the Church, as the dominant power in Europe, was responsible for many matters that are now the concern of the secular authorities. One of the most important of these was education; and among the achievements most frequently claimed for Christianity is that it kept learning alive in the monasteries after the barbarian conquest of Rome. The claim is justified in a sense, but it has as its inevitable corollary that outside the monasteries the Church allowed learning to die.

The victorious barbarians embraced Christianity with surprising readiness, and it is reasonable to suppose that they would have taken no less readily to education if the Church had provided it. But it did not. The Empire before its conversion had been well provided with schools, but as they were mainly concerned with the study of pagan literature they were considered unsuitable for the education of Christians, and those of them that were not swept away in the debacle of the barbarian invasion were allowed to fall out of use. They were replaced, when they were replaced, by monastery and cathedral schools which admitted only boys who intended to enter the Church.

The only serious attempt to provide lay education in the Dark Ages was initiated by the Emperor Charlemagne who, though himself barely literate, had a great respect for culture and learning. He founded a school at Aachen, later known as the School of the Palace, and put pressure on bishops and abbots to establish similar schools elsewhere in his realm, and to open such monastery and cathedral schools as already existed to students who did not intend to become priests or monks. For a time it seemed that a small flame of learning was beginning to flicker through the murk of the Dark Ages. But it was only Charlemagne's influence that kept it alive; it sank down after his death. The Church had no real interest in educating the laity, and for two centuries or more the son of a prince in Christian Europe had (unless he entered the Church) less chance of becoming literate than the son of a slave in imperial Rome.*

In the Middle Ages boys of good family received their education by being sent at an early age to serve as pages in noble households, where they acquired a modicum of book-learning and were initiated into the code of chivalric behaviour. Working people, with few exceptions, remained illiterate, their education being confined to the skills and crafts of their occupation. There were, however, a few parish schools which gave instruction in Latin and religion, and from them in the eleventh and twelfth centuries developed the first grammar schools, with a wider curriculum which included rhetoric, logic and mathematics.

The Renaissance brought a great explosion of intellectual activity and an upsurge of interest in the classical, pagan world: and education, though still largely under

* This statement must be qualified as regards England, where—largely through the activities of the Venerable Bede and Alfred the Great in the eighth and ninth centuries—the standard of literacy was higher than elsewhere in Europe.

the control of the Church, became more widespread and
less restricted in content. But in most European countries
it remained the preserve of a privileged class. Even as late
as the beginning of the nineteenth century, nine-tenths of
Christian Europe was illiterate.

The situation in England at that time was reasonably
typical of that in Western Europe as a whole. The only
education available to the children of the poor (and that
to no more than a tiny minority) was provided by
Sunday schools and a few so-called 'charity schools'. The
curriculum of these schools consisted almost entirely of
reading and religious instruction; there was a general
feeling that a wider education was not only unnecessary
but might well make the working classes discontented
with their lot. However, 'liberal' ideas were beginning to
stir, and in 1807 Samuel Whitbread introduced into the
Commons a Bill to establish state-aided schools providing
two years' education for poor children. But the Bill was
thrown out by the Lords owing to the united opposition
of the Bench of Bishops, led by the Archbishop of
Canterbury, who protested that the Bill would go far 'to
subvert the first principles of education in this country,
which had hitherto been, and he trusted would continue
to be, under the control of the establishment'. The establishment, it appeared, still had little more enthusiasm for
popular education than it had had in the ages of faith.
However the extension of educational opportunity was
clearly in the air, so the churches, bowing to the inevitable,
resolved that it should at least be extended under their
auspices. The first to move were in fact the Nonconformists, who in 1808 established the British and Foreign
Schools Society, and in 1811 the Church of England
followed suit with the foundation of the National Society

'for promoting the education of the poor in the principles of the Established Church'.

In the years that followed, these two societies—aided, from 1833 onwards, by substantial annual grants from the exchequer—were responsible for the establishment of elementary or 'national' schools in many parts of the country. These schools left much to be desired: the curriculum was narrow, the teaching methods primitive (consisting largely of mechanical rote memorizing under the supervision of 'monitors' aged about 14), and the buildings grim and insanitary. In 1861 an Education Commission reported that 'the schools were generally in a deplorable state in most parts of Britain'; and in the century that followed, despite the resistance and delaying tactics of the establishment, responsibility for popular education was progressively transferred from the Church to the State.

In 1870 our present far-reaching system of State education was inaugurated by the Forster Education Act, under which all children between the ages of five and ten years were required to attend school. Local School Boards were appointed to establish new schools, known as Board Schools, in areas where no Church school existed; and whenever a Church school closed—and the buildings of many of them were in such disrepair as to be fit only for immediate demolition—a Board school was erected to replace it. These schools at first made a nominal charge, but in 1891 they were made free by law. In 1902 the School Boards were replaced by Local Education Authorities, who were responsible for secondary and technical as well as for elementary education.

By the Act of 1870 it was decreed that religious instruction, which in Church schools was given in accordance with the denomination to which the school belonged, should in the Board schools be non-denominational—in the sense that, in the words of the Act, 'no religious catechism or religious formulary which is distinctive of any particular denomination shall be taught'. When free secondary education was later established this distinction was maintained, and many Local Education Authorities produced—and are still producing—'agreed syllabuses' for non-denominational religious instruction.

Thus was inaugurated the so-called 'dual system' of Church schools and State schools existing side by side—a system that is still with us, to the extent that at the time of writing one child in five in England and Wales spends some part of his school life in a Church school. Since the turn of the century, the policy of the State towards Church schools has been to give steadily increasing amounts of financial assistance in return for increased administrative control. But there is a growing feeling today that the dual system has outlived whatever usefulness it had, and that the Church schools should now be brought completely within the State educational system.

Church schools are sometimes defended on the hard-headed ground that they involve a saving to the taxpayer, but this argument is not as strong as is often supposed. However, before dealing with this point it may be well to outline briefly the present position of Church schools in our educational system, since few people are entirely clear about the now rather complex set-up.

Most Church schools, as has been said, were erected with the aid of building grants from the State: but once the buildings were up, the Churches, to begin with, were entirely responsible for paying the running costs of the schools and for keeping the buildings in repair. Since 1902, however, a series of legislative enactments has enabled them to shift a steadily increasing proportion of the financial burden on to the taxpayer. Today all Church schools have the whole of their running costs, including teachers' salaries, paid by the State. But in respect of capital cost (i.e. the cost of maintaining, and in some cases erecting, the buildings) Church schools, since the Butler Act of 1944, have been divided into two categories known as 'controlled' and 'aided'. Controlled schools receive all their maintenance costs from the State, in return for giving up part of their denominational character; aided schools provide a proportion (now fixed at 20 per cent) of their own maintenance costs, in return for which they are enabled to preserve an atmosphere considerably more 'churchy' than that of the controlled schools. In the words of the Bishop of Kingston-on-Thames, in the aided school 'the timetable can be soaked in Christianity'.[1]

From the administrative point of view, the main differences between controlled and aided schools are as follows. In controlled schools, religious instruction is based on the undenominational 'agreed syllabus' used in the State schools, though with the proviso that denominational religious instruction can be given for not more than two periods a week to those children whose parents desire it. In aided schools the religious instruction is entirely denominational—Anglican, Roman Catholic or, in a few cases, Nonconformist. In controlled schools two-thirds of the governing body is appointed by the Local Education Authority and one-third by the Church; in aided schools these proportions are reversed, so that the Church has the deciding voice in such matters as the selection of teachers. Roman Catholic schools, almost without exception, fall into the 'aided' category; Anglican schools are approximately equally divided between 'aided' and 'controlled'.

In 1959 and again in 1966 the provisions of the 1944 Butler Act were extended, largely as the result of pressure from the Catholic hierarchy. The maintenance grant for aided schools, originally 50 per cent, was raised first to 75 and then to 80 per cent; and furthermore—a most important concession—it was made available, not merely for the repair and upkeep of existing school buildings but for the building of entirely new schools—schools which, though erected largely at public expense, become unconditionally the property of the Church.

The economic argument for retaining Church schools is based on what is often referred to as 'the churches' 20 per cent contribution' towards their cost. But clearly this figure is quite misleading unless it is realized that it relates only to capital costs: since 1902 the churches have made no contribution whatever to the running costs of their schools. When both types of expenditure are taken into account, the proportion contributed by the churches—as has been convincingly shown by David Tribe in his National Secular Society pamphlet *The Cost of Church Schools*—is no more than $1\frac{1}{2}$ per cent.

Even so, it may be argued, this $1\frac{1}{2}$ per cent represents a substantial saving to the exchequer which, if there were no Church schools, would have to pay the entire cost of educating the children who now attend them. But even this saving is largely illusory, since the dual system has often resulted in the building of two small schools where a single large school would have been less costly and more efficient.

However, the case against Church schools does not rest mainly on economic grounds; the basic objection to them is that their primary *raison d'être* is to indoctrinate their pupils. Indoctrination can be briefly defined as presenting disputable views in the guise of established facts—or, as it has been spelled out in more detail by Professor Antony Flew, as 'the implanting, with the backing of some sort of special authority, of a firm conviction of the truth of doctrines either not known to be true or, in some cases, known to be false'.[2] Now, if a parent wants his child indoctrinated with some belief which he himself holds firmly, but which many people regard as doubtful or false, there is nothing to prevent him from carrying out the process himself; and where institutions exist to promote the belief in question, they have the right, if they can afford it, to found schools in which it is propagated. But they have no right at all, surely, to demand that these schools shall be paid for by the community. No form of one-sided indoctrination has any claim to form part of a state educational system.

State-subsidized religious indoctrination in Great Britain is no more defensible than political indoctrination in totalitarian countries. This parallel applies particularly to Roman Catholic schools, which make no secret of the fact that they are primarily indoctrination centres and only secondarily places of education. The Headmaster of Downside, one of the leading Catholic public schools, has said that 'the principal aim of the school is to train the boys in the knowledge and practice of the Catholic religion'.[3] And a Catholic educationist, A. C. F. Beales, Professor of the History of Education at King's College, University of London, has written as follows:

> [Our] basic philosophy (i.e. Catholicism) must not only be a part of education, but must be the core and

13

centre of it, and *every subject in the curriculum must be
considered as expressly an instrument for making that
philosophy prevail* [my italics] in the formation of our
children's character and beliefs.[4]

Mutatis mutandis, this is precisely the view of education
that is taken by all totalitarian systems, from Fascism to
Marxism.

In support of the present system it is sometimes argued
that Catholics pay rates and taxes like everyone else, and
so are entitled to say what type of education their children
should receive. But to this there are two answers. Firstly,
the pressure for Catholic education does not come
primarily from parents, but from the hierarchy: many
Catholic parents are quite content to send their children to
State schools. Secondly, the argument, carried to its
logical conclusion, could lead to a demand for special
schools for communists, Christian Scientists, Mormons,
Jehovah's Witnesses and the like, as well as for the sizable
minorities of Muslims and Hindus now in this country.
The fact that parents make a small contribution through
the rates and taxes to the cost of their children's education
does not imply that minority groups are entitled to opt
out of the national system, and have their children
segregated in special schools at the State's expense.

No mention has yet been made of one of the worst
dangers of sectarian segregation in schools—that it provides a seed-bed for sectarian hostility. This is all too
apparent at the time of writing in the religious war (for it
is nothing less) that is being waged between Catholics and
Protestants in Northern Ireland. In the words of a leading
Catholic MP, Mr Norman St John-Stevas, now Under-
Secretary of State for Education and Science: 'The

underlying divisions of Northern Ireland are not so much political as social, tribal, and religious, and they all meet and focus in the educational system, which is rigidly segregated along Catholic-Protestant lines. If this educational apartheid could be modified or got rid of altogether more would be done for peace and unity in Northern Ireland than by all the well-intentioned moves of Westminster politicians.'[5]

The abolition of Church schools, or rather their full integration into the State educational system, is one of the principal policy aims of the two main Humanist organizations in Great Britain, the British Humanist Association and the National Secular Society, and in this matter they have the support of many Christians. But abolishing Church schools would not in itself put an end to religious indoctrination, since the State schools also are compelled by law to give regular religious instruction and to begin each day with an act of worship—though a conscience clause allows children to be withdrawn from either or both if their parents require it. Humanist policy is that the act of worship should be discontinued, or at least made entirely voluntary, and that religious instruction, which today is usually just a synonym for Christian indoctrination, should be replaced by objective teaching *about* Christianity (and probably, in the higher forms, about other world religions as well) and by moral training on basically secular lines.

Some Humanists, though they support the above policy in principle, are inclined to feel that 'RI' and acts of worship are now little more than harmless anachronisms, and that getting rid of them, though doubtless desirable, is hardly an urgent priority. And it is probably true that with many—possibly most—children today much of the indoctrination they receive goes in at one ear and out at the other (which is quite the best thing it can do), so that 'RI' for them is no more than a waste of time. But to the children (often the most thoughtful and sensitive) who take the instruction seriously, it can be a potent source of intellectual confusion and emotional disturbance. And it encourages (again in those who take it seriously) an attitude of passive credulity that is wholly foreign to the educational ideals of today.

Christian educationists will probably argue that the doctrinal content of 'RI' has now been reduced to a minimum. And it is true that many Local Education Authorities, largely as a reaction to Humanist pressure, have drastically revised their Agreed Syllabuses in recent years. But even the most 'advanced' of these syllabuses (and I have examined a number of them), though they play down heaven and hell, soft-pedal on the virgin birth and the miracles, and make extensive use of the term 'symbolic', still assume without question the truth of the basic Christian dogmas of the existence of God, the divinity of Jesus, and the life after death. And these, in the terms of the definition of indoctrination given above, are not established facts but disputable (and widely disputed) opinions.

It is also sometimes argued, at all events by Anglicans, that they are not 'really' indoctrinating, but simply giving children the information and the experience that are necessary if they are later to make an informed choice between Christianity and other world-views. But those who take this line would be unlikely, one imagines, to accept a parallel argument if it were used by a Communist—i.e. that bringing up a child as a Marxist is the best way to ensure that he will later make an informed choice between Communism and other political philosophies.

Indoctrination in schools is not confined to the 'RI' class; it is involved even more obviously in the act of worship. In the daily assembly, praise and thanks are offered to God and Jesus, and supplicatory prayers, asking for grace, forgiveness and sometimes for more material benefits, are addressed to them. Clearly all this would be play-acting unless the supernatural beings invoked did in fact exist, and were in a position to grant requests and to appreciate homage. A Christian educationist made the same point from the opposite angle when he wrote in a pamphlet issued by the Society for the Propagation of Christian Knowledge, 'An act of worship communicates religious truths more powerfully than any kind of direct religious instruction ... because the truths are implicit rather than explicit, because in fact they are simply taken for granted.'[6]

But why should children be encouraged to 'take for granted' beliefs that are questioned, if not rejected outright, by most educated people today? The answer commonly is, for the sake of their morals. But there is surely something paradoxical in trying to promote truthfulness and other virtues among children by teaching them things that are not true. Humanists are keenly aware of the importance of moral training, but they regard the attempt to base it on supernatural religion as both misguided and dangerous.

However, Education Ministers from both parties have supported this policy. Sir David Eccles, who was Conservative Minister of Education under Harold Macmillan, said in a Parliamentary debate in 1961:

Let us consider the background of a large number of the children in the schools to-day. Their parents may be decent people who behave well to each other, keep their promises, and help their neighbours, and they do all this because their own parents handed on to them the tradition of Christian morality. But they may not be members of any Church. They are simply living on the capital of those who were. These children see the parents behaving well, but no one tells them why, and it seems to me that religious instruction can make explicit to these children why such good behaviour is right and why the contrary would be wrong. . . .

I can but repeat my conviction that in this generation, when we have somewhat lost our faith, we must turn to the schools and ask them to accept the challenge to become the instruments for recovery and renewal.

Soon after the delivery of this speech, a group of Humanist teachers attending a Conference of Educational Associations passed the following resolution, which was sent to the Minister:

We deplore the view expressed by the Minister of Education that moral behaviour and a regard for moral standards are a function of Christian belief and are promoted only by Christian teachings and example, acknowledged and unacknowledged. As non-Christians we resent this view as prejudiced and, on the evidence, absurd. Moreover we think that it is contrary to the public interest to spread the idea that social morality is dependent upon beliefs which only convinced Christians can hold.

However, seven years later the Minister of State for Education and Science in the Labour government, Mr

Edward Short, was expressing basically the same view as Sir David. Having urged Christians of all denominations to 'man the barricades' to resist any attempt to remove 'RI' from the curriculum, he later elaborated his views in a TV discussion which was published in the *Listener*.

It was clear from this discussion that Mr Short himself was by no means an orthodox Christian; when he was questioned about his own religious views he would commit himself to nothing more definite than that there was 'an ultimate reality of some kind behind the material world' and that God was 'a reasonable hypothesis'. But he had no misgivings about teaching children that the existence of God was an unquestioned fact. 'Young people may reject it later in life, but I think this basic dogma, if it is a dogma, must be put across'—the reason being, apparently, that it would 'help young people to enrich their personal lives' and 'give them a moral basis for living with other people'.[7]

The assumption behind this attitude seems to be that moral principles are best erected on a substructure of religious belief, and that if later the substructure decays the morals will stand on their own. But this seems highly improbable; what is surely more likely is that if the child is brought up to assume that moral obligation and Christian belief are in some way inseparably connected, and he later discards the Christian belief, he will—to change the metaphor—throw out the moral baby with the mythological bathwater.

We are often told that the high delinquency rate today provides disturbing evidence of what happens when religious belief declines. And there may well be some truth in the view that the two tendencies are connected. But there is no truth at all, I suggest, in the inference commonly drawn—namely that the best way to reduce delinquency is to step up religious indoctrination. What we are now seeing is the breakdown of the attempt to found moral training on mythology; and we are faced with the urgent task of finding an alternative and less precarious basis. This need is now increasingly recognized, and at the time of writing many individual psychologists and educationists, and at least two organizations—the Social Morality Council and the Schools Council Moral Education Curriculum Unit*—are working actively on the problem of how best to conduct moral education along secular lines.

It is not without significance that the section of the population among whom moral training is most closely bound up with religion—namely the Roman Catholics— has a delinquency rate two to three times that of the population in general.† When this fact was first widely

* This organization has pioneered the production of a number of books and pamphlets (known collectively as *Lifeline*, and individually bearing such titles as 'What Would You Have Done?' and 'In Other People's Shoes'), which can be used, in school or out, as a basis for discussion on problems of conduct and personal relationships.

† Figures supporting this statement are available from many countries besides Britain—in particular from the United States, Australia and Holland. But most of these figures are twenty years old or more: up-to-date information is becoming increasingly difficult to obtain, for reasons which (to quote Professor Flew) 'we can only, but may easily, guess'.

Some of the most recent figures available for Britain are as follows. In 1953 one of my colleagues in Aberdeen University obtained from the Home Office figures for 'the religions professed by the persons detained in prisons and Borstal institutions in England and Wales in the middle of 1952'. These showed that Roman Catholics, who then numbered about 8 per cent of the population, provided nearly 25 per cent of the detainees. In 1957 the Scottish Home Department supplied similar figures showing that in that year 40 per cent of all prison and 36 per cent of all Borstal admissions were publicized Catholics were inclined to deny it, but today they do not so much dispute the figures as try to explain them away. The explanation most often suggested is that the high Catholic delinquency rate is due mainly to social factors such as poverty—an explanation that has undoubtedly some validity where Britain and America are concerned. It cannot, however, explain the differences found in countries like Australia and Holland, where the economic status of Catholics is little, if at all, lower than that of other sections of the community.

Another suggested explanation is that most of the delinquent Catholics must be lapsed Catholics—i.e. people who have been baptized into the Church and so still appear as Catholics on the records, but who in fact have lapsed from their faith. There may well be some truth in this; but if the high delinquency rate among baptized

---

of Catholics, as compared with about 15 per cent of Catholics for the whole population of Scotland. Since that time, however, requests for information have been met by the Home Office with the reply that 'this data (*sic*) is not collected and processed centrally and is not, therefore, available'.

A few non-official figures may be quoted, however. A book by J. Trenaman published in 1952 and entitled *Out of Step* showed that in the army during the war delinquency rates among Catholics were approximately twice as high as among non-Catholics. In the Roman Catholic weekly *The Tablet* for 6 August 1955, the Catholic chaplain of Holloway Prison revealed that the proportion of Catholics in that institution was about 20 per cent. In the *Catholic Herald* for 30 October 1964 appeared the statement, 'social workers have racked their brains for years to try to find out why the approved schools have such a high proportion of Catholic children—a quarter of the whole'. And in *The Tablet* for 3 November 1973 the director of ROMA (Rehabilitation of Metropolitan Addicts), himself a Catholic, drew attention to the high proportion of Catholics among alcoholics and drug addicts. He wrote, 'I must know more than 200 registered addicts in London, and although I cannot give a precise figure I have the impression that at least 50 per cent are Catholics'.

Catholics is indeed due largely to the minority who have lapsed, this implies that the delinquency rate among lapsed Catholics must be very high indeed.* One would not wish to press the point that two of the greatest evildoers of this century—Hitler and Goebbels—were lapsed Catholics, while Stalin was a lapsed seminarian of the Georgian Orthodox Church. But the fact, if it is a fact, that lapsed Catholics are quite exceptionally prone to crime surely supports the view that those who are taught that morals depend on religion, and who later discard the religion, often discard the morals as well.

There can be no doubt that increasing numbers of young people, Protestants as well as Catholics, are now rejecting supernatural Christianity. The extent to which this is happening in the most intellectual stratum— namely sixth-form grammar school pupils, who are likely to be the opinion-formers of the next generation— has been shown by a recent opinion survey.[8] A questionnaire on moral and religious beliefs was given to some two thousand sixth-formers in 1963, and again to a closely similar group in 1970. Thus it was possible to see how far opinion had changed over the seven-year period. The questionnaire was concerned mainly with moral attitudes, but it also included questions about religious beliefs, in particular about the existence of God and the divinity of Jesus. Pupils were asked to indicate their degree of belief or disbelief on the familiar five-point scale of 'Firmly

* To elucidate this point, let us make the assumption (oversimplified for the sake of argument) that in a group of 8,000 baptized Catholics, 2,000 have lapsed and 100 have committed crimes. Then the proportion of criminals in the total group is, of course, 1 in 80. But if the majority (say 80) of the 100 criminals belonged to the sub-group of 2,000 lapsed Catholics, the proportion of criminals in this sub-group would be 1 in 25.

believe: believe: don't know: disbelieve: firmly disbelieve.' If all who believed (though not necessarily
'firmly') both in the existence of God and the divinity of
Jesus are classed as Christians, the enquiry showed that
over the seven-year period the proportion of Christians
declined from just under half (49.8%) to just over a third
(33.6%). The boys, as seems invariably the case, were
more sceptical than the girls; separate figures for the two
sexes showed a decline from 37% to 25% among boys,
and from 63% to 42% among girls. The decline is likely
to have continued after the pupils left school, at all events
among those who went on to the University; an enquiry
on a smaller scale conducted at Edinburgh University in
1960 showed the proportion of believers decreasing
steadily from the first year to the fourth.[9]

Increasing scepticism about the truth of the Gospels,
however, is not the only reason why it is undesirable to
use them as a basis for moral training. Christianity—that
harsh, joyless, guilt-obsessed religion that makes happiness
so suspect and virtue so unattractive—has far less to offer
than has Humanism, whether of the pre-Christian or the
post-Christian kind. The ethic of present-day Humanism
has already been expounded (Chapter 2); but if we are to
seek moral inspiration mainly in the literature of the past,
then the philosophic writers of classical Greece and Rome
present an ethic that is far loftier, and far more appealing,
than that of the Gospels. Paganism, as has been well said,
walks on the sunny side of the world; Christianity walks
on the dark side. Christianity has almost nothing of the
sunlit serenity—the 'light, sane joy of life'—to be found
in the best of the pagans. Where Jesus disparaged earthly
life and the human affections, and said 'Woe unto you
that laugh,' Epicurus, in the fourth century BC, said

'Friendship goes dancing round the world proclaiming to us all to awake to the praises of a happy life.'[10] Where Christianity exalted suffering, Epicurus said 'We call pleasure the beginning and end of the blessed life'— adding, however: 'But when we maintain that pleasure is the end, we do not mean the pleasures of profligates and those that consist in sensuality ... but freedom from pain in the body and from trouble in the mind. For it is not continuous drinkings and revellings, nor the satisfaction of lusts, nor the enjoyment of luxuries which produce a pleasant life, but sober reasoning, searching out the motives for all choice and avoidance, and banishing mere opinions, to which are due the greatest disturbance of the spirit.'[11]

This is all very well, some Christians may say, but it has not much to do with morality. But when they are dealing specifically with questions of conduct the pre-Christian Humanists, without the aid of threats and denunciations, are often far more persuasive than the Gospels. Some Stoic pronouncements have already been cited (pp. 28–30), and I shall now quote a few more. Epictetus, a former slave who became a teacher of philosophy in Rome in the first century AD said 'Let no wise man estrange himself from the government of the state; for it is both impious to withdraw from being useful to those that need it, and cowardly to give way to the worthless. For it is foolish to choose rather to be governed ill, than to govern well.'[12] Compare this with the Christian Tertullian's statement 'Nothing is of less interest to us than public affairs.' Among other reported sayings of Epictetus are—'If any one tells you that such a person speaks ill of you, do not make excuses about what is said of you, but answer: "He doth not know my other faults, else he would not have mentioned only these'':'[13] and again 'As the sun doth not wait for prayers and incantations to be prevailed on to rise, but immediately shines forth, and is received with universal salutation: so, neither do you wait for applauses and shouts and praises in order to do good; but be a voluntary benefactor, and you will be beloved like the sun.'[14]

It is not only the Greek and Roman moralists who compare favourably with the Christians. The philosophy of Confucius (6th century BC) has already been mentioned (pp. 27): I now quote from the *Analects*:

> Tzu-Chang asked, What must a man do, that he may thereby be fitted to govern the land? The Master said, He must pay attention to the Five Lovely Things and put away from him the Four Ugly Things. Tzu-Chang said, What are they, that you call the Five Lovely Things? The Master said, A gentleman can be bounteous without extravagance, can get work out of people without arousing resentment, has longings but is never covetous, is proud but never insolent, inspires awe but is never ferocious. . . .
>
> Tzu-Chang said, What are they, that you call the Four Ugly Things? The Master said, Putting men to death without having taught them [the right]; that is called savagery. Expecting the completion of tasks, without giving due warning; this is called oppression. To be dilatory about giving orders, but to expect absolute punctuality, that is called being a tormentor. And similarly, though meaning to let a man have something, to be grudging about bringing it out from within, that is called behaving like a petty functionary.[15]

How much more civilized is this than the sermon on the mount, with its three references to hell. And how much more relevant to the world of today—as can be said also of the writings of Confucius' contemporary, the slave Aesop, some of whose fables (such as that of the sun, the wind and the traveller's cloak and of the snake that bit on the file), contain as much moral wisdom as any of the parables in the Gospels.

The Gospel ethic, with its negative, passive, masochistic character and its obsession with suffering and sacrifice, cannot be expected to hold much appeal for children. Injunctions to resist not evil and to turn the other cheek, and pronouncements like 'blessed are the meek' and 'blessed are the poor in spirit', will make a healthy child's gorge rise. More than this, they will tend to create a most undesirable association between the ideas of goodness and soppiness—an association which, once firmly established in the mind of an adventurous child, could well lead him towards delinquency.

The ill-effects of 'RI' are intellectual as well as moral. A child of normal intelligence will inevitably be puzzled by the contradictions between what he is taught and his own experience. He is told that God is all-good and all-powerful—why then, the child wonders, did he let the boy next door get polio? Why did he allow an earthquake to kill thousands of people? He is told that God made, and loves, everything that lives. But if he loves all the animals, the child thinks, why did he arrange that they should have to kill one another for food? If he is taken to church, the child hears that death is the gateway to eternal life and should be welcomed rather than shunned; but in the real world he sees death regarded as the greatest of all evils and everything possible done to postpone it. If he asks questions he gets embarrassed, evasive answers—conveying, possibly, the suggestion that there are mysteries too deep and too sacred for our finite minds to grasp. Thus he is introduced to a realm of thought in which nothing means quite what it says, in which no statement can be taken at its face value and no line of thought followed to its logical conclusion. And this is an unwholesome intellectual climate for the future citizen of a free democracy.

In this era of mass communication and propaganda there is a need, probably greater than at any time in history, for people who set a high value on veracity; people who do not accept uncritically everything they read or are told, and who, if they find that their ideas on some subject are in a state of confusion, try to clear the confusion up. But religious training encourages the opposite mental attitude—the attitude that regards intellectual confusion and discomfort as the normal human condition, and suspects lucidity as a sign of shallowness. It is all too easy for us to think we are being profound when we are just being muddled, and to pride ourselves on our broadmindedness because the opinions we hold contradict one another. But these are tendencies that it is the business of education to discourage, not to foster.

We have still to consider what is perhaps the commonest argument used for retaining 'RI'—that the parents want it. And it is true that the results of several opinion polls seem to support this contention. But most of these polls are open to serious criticism regarding the wording of the questions. The most flagrant example was a questionnaire circulated in Durham and Newcastle in 1966,[16] which was claimed to show an enormous majority against change. The claim was based mainly on the answers to the question 'Do you want your child to know about and understand Christianity?'—to which over 90 per cent replied 'Yes'. If the question had been asked of a group of Humanists the figure would probably have been nearer 100 per cent. Humanists, almost without exception, want their children to 'know about and understand Christianity'; but this is very different from wanting them indoctrinated with Christian belief.

The same objection applies in lesser degree to all polls so far conducted on this subject. None of them has indicated whether 'religious instruction' is to be understood as Christian indoctrination or as teaching *about* Christianity, and no firm conclusion about parents' views can be drawn until we have a poll which makes this important distinction clear. In fact, however, there is good reason to suppose that what parents most want for their children is neither of these things, but simply moral training—and that most of those who support 'RI' do so because they have been led to suppose that moral and religious education are inseparable.

This view about parental attitudes is strongly supported by an enquiry conducted in 1969 by National Opinion Polls on behalf of the British Humanist Association. The questionnaire listed eight aims or objectives which might reasonably be felt to be important in education—such as training for a career, encouraging participation in politics and local affairs, developing a sense of right and wrong, and developing Christian conviction—and parents were asked to say which of these aims they considered most important. Top of the list was training for a career, put first by 40 per cent. Next came developing a sense of right and wrong, put first by 25 per cent. Developing Christian conviction was put first by 5 per cent of those aged 65 and over, and 2 per cent of those under 45. Thus it is clear that parents today—particularly younger parents

—attach far more importance to moral training than to doctrinal instruction. What is needed now is an opinion poll which frankly confronts them with the fact that the two things can be separated, and which explores their reaction to the suggestion that moral education should be given along secular lines.

In conclusion, it is necessary to correct two common misconceptions about the Humanist attitude to 'RI'. Humanists are opposed to Christian indoctrination, but they are emphatically not opposed to objective teaching *about* the Christian religion. This is an essential part of a liberal education; without some knowledge of the basic doctrines and the history of Christianity it would be impossible to understand much of European literature, history and art. Moreover, the Christian stories—highly unedifying though some of them are—are part of our cultural heritage, as are other mythological stories such as those of St George and the dragon and the knights of the round table. The child should certainly hear them; but he should hear them *as* stories, not as something which it is his duty to try to believe.

The second misconception is to suppose that Humanists want to replace Christian indoctrination with Humanist indoctrination in the schools. This is far from the truth. Humanists are opposed to indoctrination in any form—what they ask of the schools is neutrality. There is no ground whatever for the suggestion that if Humanists had their way, Christian teachers would be obliged to conceal their beliefs from their pupils. It is an excellent thing, in the Humanist view, for children to encounter a wide variety of opinions on religion, politics and all other controversial issues that interest them. But they should encounter them *as* opinions, with which they are free to

14

agree or disagree; neither in religion nor in any other field should one selected opinion be presented as fact.

Milton said in the *Areopagitica*: 'Let truth and error grapple; who ever saw truth put to the worse, in free and open encounter.' Few Protestant Christians today would, one imagines, reject this statement in principle; so one may hope that before long they will be willing to accept its implications in practice.

REFERENCES

Chapter 1

1 *The Tablet*, 21 April 1956.
2 *Apologia pro Vita Sua* (1874), Part VII.

Chapter 2

1 Fontana Books (1955). This book contains three series of broadcast talks which were originally published separately under the titles *Broadcast Talks* (1942), *Christian Behaviour* (1943) and *Beyond Personality* (1944).
2 *The Humanist Outlook*, ed A. J. Ayer (1968), p. 5.
3 'Morality: Religious and Secular', *The Rationalist Annual*, 1961.
4 *The Tablet*, 20 October 1965.
5 *African Genesis* (1961), p. 81.
6 *Scientific American*, June 1961, reprinted in *Primate Social Behaviour* (Insight Books, 1963).
7 *Listener*, 5 November, 1964.
8 *Op cit.*, pp. 80–81.
9 'The Humanity of Man'. Presidential Address to the British Association reported in *The Times*, 31 August 1961.
10 In *Sex and Temperament in Three Primitive Societies* (1935).
11 In *Patterns of Culture* (1935).
12 *Epistles*, 95.
13 *On Duties*, I, 22.
14 *On Laws*, I, 43.
15 *Christianity, Past and Present* (1952), p. 81.
16 *The Tablet*, 15 November 1958.
17 *Daily Herald*, 14 January 1955.

Chapter 4

1 *The Apocrypha and Pseudepigraphia of the Old Testament in English*'
   ed. R. H. Charles (1913), Vol. II, pp. 341–2.
2 *De Ira*, I, 15.
3 *Ibid.*, II, 34.
4 *Meditations*, XI, 18.
5 *The Principles of Moral and Political Philosophy*, (1785), I, 7.
6 *On Duties*, III, 6.
7 *Meditations*, VI, 44.
8 *Apologeticus*, XXXVIII.
9 *The True Doctrine*, quoted by Origen *Contra Celsum*, trans.
   H. Chadwick, VI, 14; III, 44; I, 9.

Chapter 6

1 *Summa Theologica*, III, qu. 94.
2 Translation by Henry Bell (1651), quoted in Lecky *Rationalism in
   Europe* (1865), IV, 1.
3 *William Cowper* (1953), p. 234.
4 *The Scarlet Tree* (1946), pp. 70, 84.

Chapter 7

1 *Annals*, XV, 44.
2 *On the Deaths of the Persecutors*, Chaps. 3 and 4.
3 The entire correspondence is quoted in E. W. Barnes *The Rise of
   Christianity* (1947), pp. 307–9.
4 *The Decline and Fall of the Roman Empire* (1776–1788), Chap. 16.
5 *Ad Scapulam*, V.
6 *Meditations*, XI, 3.
7 For a description of this phenomenon, see A. H. M. Jones *Constantine and the Conversion of Europe* (1948), pp. 94–7.

Chapter 8

1 From a letter of Arius to Eusebius, Bishop of Nicomedia, quoted in A. H. M. Jones *Constantine and the Conversion of Europe* (1948) pp. 141–2.
2 *History of European Morals* (1877), Chap. 4. The principal sources on which Lecky drew in these passages, and to which he gave detailed source-references in his footnotes, were Dean Milman's *History of Christianity under the Empire* and *History of Latin Christianity*.

Chapter 9

1 Letter 108 to Eustochium trans. S. L. Greenslade, *Early Latin Theology* (Library of Christian Classics Vol. V), pp. 351, 363, 380.
2 *History of European Morals* (1877), Chap. 4.
3 Letter 22 to Eustochium, trans. F. A. Wright. *Select Letters of St Jerome* (Loeb Classical Library), pp. 67–68.
4 *Op. cit.* Chap. 4.
5 Letter 14 to Heliodorus, trans. F. A. Wright, *op. cit.*, pp. 31–2.
6 *Op. cit.* Chap. 4.
7 *Historical Memorials of Canterbury* (1885), pp. 75–6.
8 *The Life of Blessed Henry Suso*, trans. T. F. Knox (1865), Chaps. 17, 19, quoted by William James in *The Varieties of Religious Experience* (1903) pp. 307, 308, 309.
9 *Ibid.* Chap. 53.
10 Cf, for example, the chapter on Suso in J. M. Clark, *The Great German Mystics* (1949).
11 Quoted by William James in *The Varieties of Religious Experience*, p. 305. *The Collected Works of St John of the Cross* have since been translated by Kieran Kavanaugh and Otilio Rodriguez (1963).
12 Quoted by Lecky in *The Map of Life* (1899), p. 54.
13 H. D. Liddon *Life of Edward Bouverie Pusey* (1894), Vol. III, pp 100–101.
14 *Ibid.*, p. 95.

Chapter 10

1 *Gesta Francorum*, ed. Rosalind Hill (1962), pp. 91–2.

Chapter 11

1 *The Middle Ages* (1929), p. 495.
2 Quoted in the *Observer*, 3 September 1972.

Chapter 12

1 Quoted in William Sargant *Battle for the Mind* (1959), Chap. 9.
2 Quoted in Hugh Trevor-Roper 'Witches and Witchcraft,' *Encounter*, June 1967, p. 20.
3 *Daily Telegraph*, 5 November 1958.
4 *The Times*, 20 April 1972.

Chapter 13

1 Quoted in Werner Keller *Diaspora* (1971), p. 101.
2 Article 'Jews' in *Encyclopaedia Britannica*.
3 '*Von den Juden und ihren Lügen*' (1543), in *Martin Luthers Werke*, ed. Karl Drescher (1920), Vol. LIII, pp. 446, 523, 524, 526–7, 537.
4 *Martin Luther and the Birth of Protestantism* (1968), p. 320.
5 *Objections to Roman Catholicism* (1964), p. 175.
6 Quoted in Joachim Kahl *The Misery of Christianity* (1971), pp. 61–2.

Chapter 14

1 *Rationalism in Europe* (1865), Chap. 5.
2 Quoted in Werner Keller *Diaspora* (1971), p. 333.
3 *Broadcasting: Sound and TV* (1958), p. 175.

References

Chapter 15

1 *Tusculan Disputations*, II, 17.
2 *Epistulae Morales*, VII.
3 *The Divine Institutes*, trans. William Fletcher, Book VI, Chap. 20. Ante-Nicene Christian Library, Vol. XXI.
4 *De Spectaculis*, trans. T. R. Glover, in *Tertullian* (Loeb Classical Library), pp. 289, 299.
5 *History of European Morals* (1877), Chap. 4.

Chapter 16

1 *Morals in Evolution* (1915), p. 209.
2 *Woman: her Position and Influence in Ancient Greece and Rome and among the Early Christians* (1907), pp. 153–4.
3 Letter 22 to Eustochium, trans. F. A. Wright, *Select Letters of St Jerome* (Loeb Classical Library), p. 93.
4 Quoted in Lecky *Rationalism in Europe* (1865), Chap. 1.
5 *De Exhortatione Castitatis*, trans. W. P. le Saint, in *Treatises on Marriage and Remarriage*, Ancient Christian Writers Series No. 13, pp. 56–7.
6 Letter 22 to Eustochium, *op. cit.*, p. 95.
7 *The Anti-Pelagian Works of St Augustine*, ed. Marcus Dods, Vol. II. Ante-Nicene Christian Library, Vol. XII.
8 Ancient Christian Writers Series, No. 11, trans. Henry Davis, pp. 188–9.
9 *Lettres Complètes d'Abélard et d'Heloïse*, trans. M. Gréard, pp. 579–80.
10 *Patrologia Latina*, 217: 1058–9, quoted in *The Tablet*, 6 September 1968.
11 *De Monogamia*, *op. cit.*, p. 107.
12 Letter 54 to Furia, *op. cit.*, p. 233.
13 Letter 107 to Laeta, *op. cit.*, pp. 359–60, 364–5.
14 Letter 14 to Heliodorus, *op. cit.*, p. 51.
15 Letter 108 to Eustochium, trans. S. L. Greenslade, *Early Latin Theology* (Library of Christian Classics Vol. V), p. 370.
16 *History of European Morals* (1877), Chap. 4.

17 *Ibid.*, Chap. 5.

18 *Civilization* (1969), pp. 63–4.

19 *The Paston Letters*, no. 71, quoted by H. S. Bennett in *The Pastons and their England* (1922), p. 30.

20 *Ibid.*, no. 112, quoted by Bennett, *ibid.*, p. 81.

21 *Christianity and Morals* (1939), pp. 342–3.

Chapter 17

1 Westermann, W. L. *Harvard Studies in Classical Philology*, Supp. Vol. (1941), reprinted in M. I. Finley *Slavery in Classical Antiquity* (1960), pp. 25, 23.

2 Finley, M. I. *Historia* 8 (1959), reprinted in *Slavery in Classical Antiquity*, p. 68.

3 Pseudo-Xenophon, *Constitution of Athens*, I. 10. The authorship of the pamphlet is unknown, but was falsely attributed to Xenophon, with whose works it is usually printed.

4 *Life and Leisure in Ancient Rome* (1969), pp. 111, 112, 113.

5 *De Clementia*, I, 18.

6 *The Divine Institutes*, trans. William Fletcher, Book V, Chap. 16. Ante-Nicene Christian Library, Vol. XXI.

7 *History of Europe* (1935), Chap. 23.

8 Quoted in G. M. Trevelyan *British History in the Nineteenth Century and After* (1937), p. 53.

9 *English Social History* (1942), p. 495.

10 Quoted in Emil Ludwig *Lincoln* (1930), pp. 170–1.

11 Matthews, D. G. *Slavery and Methodism: a Chapter in American Morality 1780–1845* (1965), pp. 73–4.

12 *Biblical Repertory and Theological Review*, Vols. VIII and X quoted in Lorman Ratner *Powder Keg: Northern Opposition to the Antislavery Movement* (1968), p. 92.

Chapter 18

1 *Milton's God* (1961), pp. 254–5.

2 'Humanity's Gain from Unbelief', in *Champion of Liberty: Charles Bradlaugh*, Centenary Volume 1933, p. 144.

3 *Religion Today* (1969), pp. 4–5.
4 *Suggestions for Thought to the Searchers after Truth among the Artizans of England* (1859), Vol. I, p. 262. This book is now extremely rare, and those who wish to consult it must go to the library of the British Museum. But references to it, and to Florenec Nightingale's religious opinions, are made (albeit cautiously) in the short life of Florence Nightingale in Lytton Strachey's *Eminent Victorians*, and in Cecil Woodham-Smith's monumental biography.
5 Review (*Listener*, 6 March 1958) of Liv Nansen Hoyer *Nansen: A Family Portrait* (1957).
6 *Suggestio Falsi*, 29 December 1961.

Chapter 19

1 Quoted in Paul Blanshard *Freedom and Catholic Power* (1952), p. 270.
2 *The Documents of Vatican II*, ed. Walter M. Abbott S.J. (1966), p. 679, and *The Times*, 22 September 1965.
3 *The Times*, 22 September 1965.
4 *The Documents of Vatican II*, pp. 346, 348.
5 Patrick A. Finney *Moral Problems in Hospital Practice* (1947), p. 60, quoted in Paul Blanshard, *op. cit.*, p. 107.
6 Elizabeth Pakenham (ed.), *Catholic Approaches* (1955), p. 117.
7 *Observer Colour Supplement*, 18 January 1970.
8 *Observer*, 3 June 1956.
9 *Listener*, 8 July 1954.
10 *Observer*, 3 January 1960.
11 *The Linacre Quarterly* (official Journal of the Federation of Catholic Physicians' Guilds), January 1947, quoted in Paul Blanshard, *op. cit.*, p. 143.
12 *New York Times*, 19 August 1947, quoted in Paul Blanshard, *op. cit.*, p. 119.
13 *Journal of a Soul*, trans. Dorothy White (1965), p. 37.
14 Elizabeth Pakenham *op. cit.*, p. 20.
15 J. H. Rose, *The Personality of Napoleon* (1912), pp. 127–8.
16 *The Tablet*, 28 January 1967.
17 Monica Lawlor *Out of this World* (1965), pp. 16–17, 62–3, 130.

18 Quoted in *The Tablet*, 18 September 1971.

19 *Journal of a Soul*, trans. Dorothy White (1965), pp. 67–8.

Chapter 20

1 *History of European Morals* (1877), Chap. 4.

1 *Doctrine in the Church of England* (1938), pp. 37–8.

2 *The Times*, 17 May 1969.

3 *Apologia pro Vita Sua* (1864), Part V.

4 *Op. cit.*, pp. 204–5.

5 *On Compromise* (1874), Chap. 3.

Chapter 21

1 *The Times Educational Supplement*, 12 January 1968.

2 'Against Indoctrination' in *The Humanist Outlook*, ed. A. J. Ayer (1968), p. 80.

3 *Queen*, July 1970.

4 *Looking Forward in Education*, ed. A. V. Judges (1955), p. 84.

5 *Sunday Express*, 14 May 1972.

6 J. G. Williams, *Leading School Worship*, p. 6.

7 *Listener*, 11 July 1968.

8 Derek Wright 'Changes in Moral and Religious Beliefs among Adolescent Boys and Girls'. Unpublished paper presented to the British Psychological Society, 1971.

9 *Edinburgh Evening News*, 25 January 1960.

10 *Fragments*, 52.

11 *Letter to Menoeceus*, 131–2.

12 *Fragments*, 126.

13 *Manual*, 33.

14 *Fragments*, 83.

15 *Analects*, trans. Arthur Waley, XX, 2.

16 P. R. May and D. R. Johnston 'Parental Attitudes to Religious Education in State Schools' *Durham Research Review*, April 1967.

INDEX